Jago Pakistan/ Wake Up, Pakistan

The Report of The Century Foundation
International Working Group on Pakistan

Thomas R. Pickering
Working Group Chair

The Century Foundation Press • New York

About The Century Foundation

The Century Foundation seeks to foster opportunity, reduce inequality, and promote security at home and abroad.

Founded in 1919 by the progressive business leader Edward Filene, the Foundation pursues its mission by conducting timely, nonpartisan research and policy analysis that informs citizens, guides policymakers, and reshapes what government does for the better.

Over its nearly century-long history, the Foundation has been on the forefront of positive change in some of the most critical areas of domestic and foreign policy, including the promotion of equality of educational opportunity, the strengthening of economic security, the protection of workers and consumers, the empowerment of voters, and the fostering of international peace and security.

The Foundation is based in New York, with a satellite office in Washington, D.C. Its fellows come from academia, journalism, and public service, but share a commitment to the Foundation's abiding belief in the power of ideas.

Library of Congress Cataloguing-in-Publication Data
available on request from the publisher

Manufactured in the United States of America

Cover design by Abigail Grimshaw
Text design by Cynthia Stock

Contents

Preface

In 2009, when The Century Foundation assembled an international task force to study the prospects for a negotiated political settlement to the war in Afghanistan, the debate over the course of that conflict dominated political and security discussions worldwide, to say nothing of how it was perceived throughout South Asia. Six years later, the U.S. and North Atlantic Treaty Alliance (NATO) presence in Afghanistan has decreased significantly, and the nature of the mission has changed, from directly combatting an insurgency to supporting a new government.

Global attention has since shifted further afield. The initial optimism of the Arab uprisings of 2011 has given way to resurgent authoritarianism and militancy, and much of the Middle East is now beset by instability and violence. P5+1 negotiations with Iran over its nuclear program continue to focus the attention of the international community. Tensions with Russia over Ukraine and the future of the U.S. role in the Asia-Pacific are but two issues that increasingly garner the focus of key policymakers.

While these events have overshadowed recent developments in South Asia, this does not translate into a diminution of the importance of the region. Upon the completion of our Afghanistan project, Ambassador Thomas Pickering, co-chair of that task force, noted that many of the issues feeding the conflict in Afghanistan were interlinked with Pakistan and that a subsequent project focused on Pakistan and the international community's engagement with it would be an important contribution.

From this initial prompting, we sought to compile a diverse group of experts—American, Pakistani, and international—to contribute to this effort. In distinction from the traditional formula for such working group reports, this effort sought to harmonize the views of Pakistanis with those of their international interlocutors as opposed to lecturing Pakistan about its many problems.

Over the course of two years, this Working Group has taken as its point of reference the transitions taking place in the region, which provide an opportunity for transcending intractable policy dilemmas. This report acknowledges frankly the severe problems facing Pakistan, many of them self-inflicted or exacerbated by conflict and political misman-agement: internal militancy, long-standing rivalries with neighbors, and struggles with economic and human development. While acknowledging the basic resilience of Pakistani society, this report warns that time is running out for critical changes to be made. It is our hope that such a call may provide a strong impetus for reform in Islamabad.

A preponderant focus on security and counterterrorism by critical players in the international community has crowded out opportunities to focus on a wider vision for engagement in the region, to the detriment not only of respective national interests of the international community but also, in many ways, the health of Pakistani democracy. Concerted diplomatic effort and attention need to be directed to this policy reorientation, and this report argues it must begin now, taking advantage of improved Afghan-Pakistani relations and the constructive engagement by China.

We are deeply grateful to the support of the Carnegie Corporation, who funded this Working Group as well as the previous Task Force on Afghanistan. Our work would be impossible without the guidance and encouragement of Carnegie Corporation president Vartan Gregorian and program director for international peace and security Stephen Del Rosso.

Within Pakistan, we wish to thank the Jinnah Institute and the Center for Research and Security Studies, two Islamabad-based research institutes that provided critical assistance during research visits by U.S. and international members of the Working Group. We are especially happy that their leaders, Ambassador Sherry Rehman and Imtiaz Gul, are among the Pakistani membership of this Working Group.

Many members of this Working Group benefited from their involvement in a U.S.-China Track II Dialogue on Afghanistan administered by Barney Rubin of New York University's Center on International Cooperation. There were numerous points of substantive intersection and that dialogue helped shape portions of this report. We appreciate those opportunities to collaborate.

The staff of The Century Foundation worked tirelessly to see this project to its completion. We owe debts of gratitude to Philip Li, our chief administrative officer and his staff for logistical and administrative support; Lucy Muirhead ably oversaw the preparations for the public events surrounding the release of this report; and Jason Renker's editorial guidance on this report was indispensable. We also owe a particular debt of gratitude to Neil Bhatiya, who helped organize the work of the group and was an integral part of the drafting and editing process.

Lastly, we are grateful to the Working Group members themselves, who have directed their substantial expertise and experience to the problems we have tried to address. We appreciate the time they have taken to undertake research trips and to contribute to and critique previous draft versions of this report.

As this report makes clear, the issues we have highlighted are long-term challenges, and the solutions to them will not be realized overnight. However, what happens in Pakistan and South Asia is critical to the future peace and prosperity of not only Pakistanis but also the international community at large.

Michael Wahid Hanna
Mosharraf Zaidi
Ambassador Robert P. Finn
Principal Investigators

Members of The Century Foundation International Working Group on Pakistan

Thomas R. Pickering, *Working Group Chair*
Vice Chairman, Hills and Company; former U.S. Under Secretary of
State for Political Affairs

Robert P. Finn, *Principal Investigator*
Non-Resident Fellow, Liechtenstein Institute on Self-Determination,
Princeton University; former U.S. Ambassador to Afghanistan

Michael Wahid Hanna, *Principal Investigator*
Senior Fellow, The Century Foundation

Mosharraf Zaidi, *Principal Investigator*
Campaign Director, Alif Ailaan

United States

Steve Coll
Dean, Columbia University Graduate School of Journalism

Cameron Munter
Professor of Practice in International Relations, Pomona College;
former U.S. Ambassador to Pakistan

Barnett Rubin
Senior Fellow and Associate Director, Afghanistan Pakistan Regional
Program, New York University Center on International Cooperation;
former Senior Adviser to the Special Representative for Afghanistan
and Pakistan in the U.S. Department of State

James Shinn
Chairman, Teneo Intelligence; CEO, Predata; Lecturer, Princeton University; former U.S. Assistant Secretary of Defense for Asian and Pacific Security Affairs

Anthony Zinni
Former Commander-in-Chief, United States Central Command

International

Richard Barrett
Senior Vice President, The Soufan Group; former head, United Nations al Qaeda and Taliban Sanctions Monitoring Team

Hikmet Çetin
Former Turkish Foreign Minister

Antje Grawe
Former Counselor, German Embassy, Pakistan

Jean-Marie Guéhenno
President, International Crisis Group

Nobuaki Tanaka
Former Japanese Ambassador to Turkey and Pakistan

Ann Wilkens
Former Chair, Swedish Committee for Afghanistan; former Swedish Ambassador to Pakistan and Afghanistan

Pakistan

Tariq Banuri
Professor in the Departments of Economics and City and Metropolitan Planning at the University of Utah

Imtiaz Gul
Executive Director, Center for Research and Security Studies

Ishrat Husain
Dean and Director of the Institute of Business Administration, Karachi

Asma Jahangir
Advocate of the Supreme Court of Pakistan; Chairperson, Human
   Rights Commission of Pakistan

Riaz Khohkar
Former Pakistani Foreign Secretary

Tariq Khosa
Former Director General, Federal Investigation Agency

Jugnu Mohsin
Publisher and Editor, *The Friday Times*

Ahmed Rashid
Journalist and author

Sherry Rehman
President and Founding Chair, Jinnah Institute; former Pakistani
   Ambassador to the United States

Najam Aziz Sethi
Editor-in-chief, *The Friday Times*

Moeed W. Yusuf
Director of South Asia Programs, United States Institute of Peace

Executive Summary

The time is long past for Pakistan to wake up to its present predicament and begin a serious reassessment of the fundamental policy challenges it faces. Decades of mistakes and misperceptions have compounded pernicious ideological choices to present Pakistani society with a series of ongoing crises it must address before its basic resilience is overwhelmed: a public sphere dominated by extremists, a crippled economy debilitated by corruption, and a deteriorating regional position. The Century Foundation International Working Group on Pakistan, comprised of a broad and diverse assemblage of American, Pakistani and international figures deeply concerned about the country's future, believes it is time for Pakistan to address these problems vigorously and comprehensively, and for its international partners to assist where they can.

1. Introduction: A Changing Pakistan

Nearly thirteen years after the U.S.-led international intervention in Afghanistan, Pakistan and the wider South Asia region are at a crossroads. While the threat from core al Qaeda has been diminished, and Afghanistan is no longer under Taliban rule, militancy in the region, especially within Pakistan proper, is still a critical and evolving threat. Additionally, as a legacy of conflict and a consequence of political mismanagement, Pakistan as a whole lags behind much of the world and most of its neighbors in many economic and human development indicators. Pakistan's political class is mired in a paralyzing fight that has crippled its legitimacy. Its perpetually strained relationship with India remains of paramount importance to regional stability. All of these issues require urgent attention and action by Pakistan's elected leaders, working with a vision shaped by Pakistanis themselves and supported by the international community. The world may face many other more seemingly immediate threats, but no country or region represents as potent a combination of complex security challenges, in addition to long-term economic and political opportunities, as do Pakistan and South Asia.

The government of Nawaz Sharif, in power for two years, has confronted several serious issues, including sustained pressure from Imran Khan's Pakistan Tehrik-e Insaf (PTI) party, whose anti-government protests attempted to challenge Sharif's legitimacy as Prime Minister. Relations between the civilian government and Pakistan's military and intelligence services have continued to be unstable since Sharif's inauguration. Disagreements between elected leaders and the military about how to understand and deal with threats facing the country impact a wide range of policy functions and imperil how the country can react to a series of profound challenges.

There is a persistent and growing intolerance of diversity—religious, ethnic, and political—that is a conceptual framework through which much of the extremism, violence and repression that dominates headlines, both from state and non-state actors, should be seen. Violence inside Pakistan—whether against the state and its agents or against religious or ethnic minorities—has grown in recent years. The horrifying attack on the Army Public School in Peshawar on December 16, 2014— the worst terror attack in Pakistan's history, which killed over 140, mostly children—was but the logical manifestation of the Pakistani Taliban's ideological war against the modern state of Pakistan. A military offensive in North Waziristan can only be considered the first step in a wider effort to contain the growth of religious extremism, a cancer which threatens Muhammad Ali Jinnah's founding vision of Pakistan. A generational struggle against such extremism is likely required, and the necessary steps need to be conceptualized now.

The economy, suffering from years of sluggish growth, is also gripped by a series of significant crises. The lack of robust regional trade, a profound skills gap driven by inadequate educational infrastructure, and the lack of basic inputs (a dependable electrical grid and government investment) have held Pakistan significantly behind its neighbors. Without a significant course correction, Pakistan risks marooning an entire generation from the modern world economy.

2. Managing Key Regional Security Challenges

After the recent optimism inspired by a relaxation of tensions between India and Pakistan, progress has stalled. The lack of an appetite for an accelerated normalization process and the domestic political costs to be confronted in pursing such in either Islamabad or New Delhi has led to a drift in the relationship, with tentative steps at meaningful interaction balanced by violence on the border and stasis on trade relations.

The relationship with Afghanistan is no less complex. While the new Afghan President, Ashraf Ghani, has prioritized good relations with Pakistan, as evidenced by a positive bilateral visit in the fall of 2014, several difficult issues continue to bedevil the relationship. Militant groups operating across the Durand Line—a border the status of which for historical and ethnic reasons Afghanistan remains opposed to—are threats to both countries. Managing the diplomatic initiative necessary to ensure momentum toward a strong bilateral relationship should be a priority for the international community, especially as relatively new players such as China expand their interaction with nations in the region. A major effort by the international community is required to sustain a diplomatic process, working with a Pakistan that matches it rhetorical clarity about the fact that a stable Afghanistan is in its best interests with sustained and concerted action.

For the region, diplomatic efforts by the international community should be concentrated on multiple tracks: regional action to improve bilateral political relationships between Pakistan and Afghanistan and Pakistan and India alike, with an additional but subsidiary focus on closer counterterrorism cooperation, and on increasing economic reforms and linkages throughout the region. An essential component of this effort is a serious normalization process between India and Pakistan. That process must address two critical security issues: the burgeoning arms race between the two nations, particularly nuclear arms, and the status of Kashmir. This will be a difficult, long-term process, but there are clearly identified confidence-building measures that can be pursued to advance an initial discussion, including realizing long-standing plans for normal trade.

3. Violent Extremism

For Pakistan, the loss of life due to internal militancy is at the point where a true policy reappraisal is necessary. The Peshawar attack must serve as the key wake-up call to an establishment that has maintained a dangerous relationship to Pakistan's vast spectrum of militant groups, lest the Sharif government squander a very powerful consensus in the wake of the attack that now is the time for decisive and immediate action. For too long, distinctions have been made between good militants and bad militants, between those who exist to serve Pakistan's foreign policy goals and those that are a direct and uncontrolled result of such policies. Politicians have also pandered to dangerous militants in return for electoral advantage and street power. The rhetorical clarity with which both elected leaders and the top ranks of the military have rejected the distinction between "good" terrorists and "bad" terrorists is very encouraging. There must not be a return to old thinking given the ample evidence of the damage such policies have done to Pakistan's interests. A comprehensive counterterrorism strategy must be a cardinal policy goal. To be effective, it should be directly connected with the renewed diplomatic efforts outlined above, and it should also move beyond large-scale military offensives in the tribal areas.

A long-term counterterrorism strategy will, additionally, build the capabilities of Pakistan's civilian law enforcement and judicial apparatus. Too often, conceptions of fighting terrorism have defaulted to a preponderant role for the Pakistani military, which in the past has led to a contradictory and ultimately self-defeating policy. If Pakistan's counterterrorism capabilities are to be sustainable and directed against all threats, it should rest on the importance of a civilian, law enforcement approach and be based on legal principles enshrined in Pakistan's constitution and international law. It should not, likewise, entirely rule out talks to disband illegal armed groups. While military pressure is put on Tehrik-i-Taliban Pakistan (TTP) operatives throughout the country, there should be a concomitant effort to develop a framework of principles for negotiations with those militant groups that may still be willing to cease violence. However, adherence to and respect for the constitution and for the fundamental rights of women and other marginalized groups must be a prerequisite for such an effort.

Effective counterterrorism policies, however, will fail without better relations between Pakistan's civilian and military leadership. The establishment of the National Security Division (NSD) is a first step in strengthening coordinated decision-making. Both the NSD and the Cabinet Committee on National Security need the resources and sustained attention of the elected leadership to fulfill their role in establishing robust systems to catalyze national security thinking between civilian and military institutions.

The terrorism challenge is just the direst among many domestic concerns confronting Pakistan. The threat of violence only further compounds the country's economic, governance, and social crises.

4. A Cooperative South Asian Economic Region

For the international community, these transitional years afford an opportunity to rethink the contours of its engagement. While counterterrorism will remain a priority of the United States, it is in neither country's interest for that to be the sole or even preponderant basis for future relations. This report advocates for an alternative frame in which regional political and economic connectivity should become the long-term goal. For the United States and the international community, the potential for South Asia to be a regional economic powerhouse is too important not to invest in moving toward this positive vision, despite clear and seemingly insuperable difficulties. Counterterrorism alone cannot be the functional basis of relations with the international community. But that approach is unlikely to change if there is not first a corresponding shift in the Pakistani state's approach to issues of extremism and militantcy.

A cooperative South Asia economic region requires improved border infrastructure and management to facilitate both cross-border trade and other linkages, including cooperative power generation and grid connections. It requires a rethinking of the trade agenda, not only bilaterally between India and Pakistan, and the region, but by the international community as well. The long-term goals of the international community's aid programs must be re-purposed to transitioning away from the breadth of its current assistance to more closely targeted aid. This will require marked improvements in the Pakistani government's ability and willingness to lead and own its development agenda. Pakistan's economic growth is directly tied to its fiscal health, which has deteriorated due to years of under-collection of taxes. The issues impacting the quality of Pakistan's governance pertain both to civic peace and to the capacity and legitimacy of the institutions of the state. The role of civic peace in promoting economic growth and that of conflict in depressing it is well known. Just as conflict leads to stagnation, stagnation exacerbates conflict. The inability of the economy to generate decent jobs in adequate numbers to absorb the growing number of young people is a sure formula for state failure.

5. Internal Governance Reform

In addition to a complex regional political and economic dynamic, exacerbated by a profound internal militancy challenge, the Pakistani state itself faces myriad challenges in administering law and order throughout its territory, aggressively expanding economic growth, providing its citizens with the human capital necessary to compete globally, and protecting the rights of minorities. Several initiatives under the broad heading of governance reform have been recommended by a variety of actors, both internal and external. While events in the region make the present propitious for shifts in regional and foreign policy, the time has also come for similar shifts in internal governance.

6. The Way Ahead: Two Post-2015 Pakistani Scenarios

As international public attention to Afghanistan dwindles with the drawdown of international military forces, there is a risk that corresponding attention to the critical issues facing Central and South Asia will not be sustained. Unless policies are adjusted to accommodate changing realities on the ground, diplomatic disengagement could have a cascading negative effect on regional trends toward stability and economic growth.

To inform the international community's approach to the way ahead, we analyze two possible scenarios for Pakistan's near term future. The first envisions an outwardly engaged Pakistan, sketching what its internal development and role in the region would look like under more optimal circumstances. It envisions a brighter future for Pakistan, in which it has tackled its extremism problem, increased the credibility and performance of governance, improved several key economic indicators, and embarked on the beginnings of regional cooperation and a comprehensive and stability-enhancing security policy. It would also entail greater trade linkages (in the region and beyond), travel and tourism, academic and informational exchanges, and increased investment flows. This progress would be matched by a renewed commitment by the international community to working with Pakistanis on mutual priorities that represent a positive and constructive series of goals for the region.

The second scenario seeks to forecast the repercussions of a continuation of the status quo, reflecting what would likely be a continued decline in security and economic benchmarks within Pakistan and a continued pattern of strained relations among nations in the region. It is instructive to consider the consequences of a policy path that looks very much like the one currently being followed for the three critical sectors of security, economy, and governance.

It is critical to understand the way in which each prospective path will have profound implications for how the international community, Pakistan, and its neighbors approach issues affecting regional progress. While the international community—NATO and, principally, the United States—is planning to transition away from the large-scale mission inside Afghanistan it has pursued for over a decade, this is not the end to the challenges that drew it in at the end of 2001. Nor is there a sufficient level of appreciation in the wider international community as to how strategically crucial the region will remain, even absent a significant western military presence.

7. Recommendations of the Working Group

It is the considered opinion of The Century Foundation International Working Group on Pakistan that Pakistan's people, particularly its elites and leaders, need to wake up to this dangerous present reality and seize the multiple opportunities Pakistan has, even if doing so contradicts dogma and slogans that have regularly substituted for serious leadership and governance. The challenges Pakistan faces must continue to be treated as a priority for the international community. Unlike previous efforts to rethink the issues facing Pakistan, this report is not the exclusive product of Western views of the country or region. The membership includes prominent Pakistanis fully cognizant of the negative trends in their own society. The recommendations also come at a time when the transitions in the region require both fresh thinking and progress on long-standing issues.

To realize the region's potential, Pakistan and the international community, including its neighbors, need to articulate a positive vision for internal reform and regional political, economic, and security cooperation, and embrace wholesale changes to implement that vision. The alternative to this vision is not just the continuation of a worrisome status quo. Rather, it is a likely acceleration of several equally problematic trends. Without movement toward the significant reforms outlined in this report, the international approach to Pakistan will not be one of constructive engagement, focused on supporting effort to maximize the country's human capital and economic opportunities. Instead, it will focus on containing what will likely be cascading violence, and the effects of the disillusionment of the next generation of Pakistanis who are ill-equipped to participate in the modern world, and whose government has done precious little to ameliorate the situation. The year 2015 introduces a unique confluence of events that offer opportunities to implement a strong course correction, opportunities that may not be available in the future.

This report catalogs a multitude of issues of concern. This Working Group realizes that none of these far-reaching changes can be achieved overnight. No single government could hope to advance all of the policy recommendations this Working Group outlines. While all require attention, there are critical recommendations which this Working Group feels must necessarily be addressed first.

In light of the daunting intergenerational set of challenges facing Pakistan this Working Group understands that sequencing is critical. Remedying structural and systemic problems, however, will be unachievable without immediate actions on Pakistan's most pressing concerns. For any chance of ultimate success at sustaining a vibrant, open, and prosperous society, Pakistan and the international community should focus their efforts on the following near-term challenges, which will serve as a springboard for the broader and systemic changes also outlined in the report:

- Arresting the scourge of violent extremism requires a holistic effort by Pakistani authorities to implement fully Prime Minster Sharif's declaration that no distinction will be made between "good" Taliban and "bad" Taliban. This must necessarily extend not just to the Taliban but to all non-state actors that threaten violence, both within and beyond Pakistan. The National Action Plan (NAP) is a welcome articulation of the national will to fight terrorism. It must be matched by a dedication of resources for its implementation not only to the military, but also to Pakistan's internal civilian law enforcement agencies and judiciary, which are also at the front of the fight. The international community can support these efforts both through bilateral initiatives, including material assistance and training, and by expanding the basis for regional cooperation.

- The Pakistani government needs urgently to invest in efforts aimed at reforming Pakistani state institutions at all levels as projected in Vision 2025, which was published in 2014 by the Planning Commission, a public policy institution within the Prime Minister's Office. Starting at the very top, from the Prime Minister's Office down through local governments, Pakistan's state institutions require reforms that engender greater confidence of citizens in the state. Without this confidence, roadmaps like Vision 2025, and recommendations like the ones in this report will struggle to accelerate economic growth (especially in the export sector), resolve undertaxation, or contribute to improvements in the generation of power and the delivery of electricity. The Prime Minister's Office and the Council of Common Interests need to work together to provide the resources to enable achievement of the government's Vision 2025. The international community must support these efforts first by focusing aid programs on the most critical areas—disaster management, education, and health—and gradually transitioning away from large-scale aid programs.

- The leadership of elected civilians in defining and executing Pakistani national security strategy is the central instrument for the formulation and implementation of a Pakistani foreign policy that can take advantage of the many regional opportunities available to Pakistan. Pakistan's maturing democratic traditions must, over time, address questions about the accountability of all publicly-funded organizations to elected leaders. The Cabinet Committee on National Security and the National Security Division represent first steps in the right direction; however, without assiduous stewardship by the top elected leaders in the country, further progress will remain elusive.

- The unprecedented cooperation between Afghanistan and Pakistan that followed President Ashraf Ghani's November 2014 visit to Islamabad presents the region with the best prospect for peace and stability in decades. Pakistan must bear in mind the very deep skepticism of Afghan public opinion about Islamabad and, as such, must implement quickly visible confidence-building measures with concrete benefits.

- The international community should use diplomatic, intelligence, and military channels to support the building relationship between the governments of Ashraf Ghani and Nawaz Sharif. Both Afghanistan and Pakistan should be encouraged to promote a "negative" symmetry deal on cross-border militant proxies, whereby Afghan authorities cease support for anti-Pakistan militants inside Afghanistan and Pakistan pledges similarly to end support for anti-Afghan elements. Pakistan should support the unity Afghan government in its efforts at a dialogue with the Afghan Taliban on reconciliation, including facilitating the direct participation of Afghan Taliban members now sheltering in Pakistan.

- The international community should encourage China's role in support of a reconciliation process in Afghanistan. The United States and China should elevate Pakistan-related discussions to a top-tier issue in their bilateral engagement, and design a framework for including Chinese participation in regional talks on counter-terrorism, counter-proliferation, and economic cooperation.

- The international community should support efforts led by India and Pakistan to restart a dialogue process, focusing especially on de-escalation along the Line of Control, the resumption of regular diplomatic consultations, and developing a framework for confidence-building measures and the expansion of non-governmental people-to-people exchanges, sporting activities, and cross-border travel.

In a world where multiple threats compete for the attention of policymakers, this report seeks to warn against neglecting a critical region that has been an ongoing source of frustration for past policymakers. Despite those difficulties, there exist possibilities for progress. Pakistan has long been seen as a resilient country, surviving a series of crises over the decades in a way that often goes underappreciated. Pakistan's people, particularly its elites and leaders, must wake up to the unique and unprecedented opportunities available to their country. Facing the serious challenges outlined in this report should represent the first steps in that direction.

CHAPTER ONE

Introduction:
A Changing Pakistan

On December 16, 2014, a shocking and brutal terrorist attack on a Peshawar school cost over 140 lives, mostly school children. The Tehrik-i-Taliban Pakistan (TTP) took immediate responsibility and promised more such attacks. It was the most chilling and highest-casualty terror attack in Pakistan's recent history. Ensconced within Pakistan's initial response to the Peshawar attack is the story of Pakistan itself. Pakistan is now in an unambiguous state of war with violent extremist groups that use terror. In the outcome of this war, the future of the country, as well as its surrounding region, hang in the balance.

For several years following the 2001 U.S.-led intervention in Afghanistan, Pakistan was among the dominant topics in global security and international development. Its large population, its proximity to Afghanistan, its long-standing conflict with India, its use of violent extremists to pursue strategic goals in the region (which it has made tentative first steps to address), its stature as the home to the world's second-largest Muslim-majority population, its expanding nuclear weapons arsenal, and its low levels of human development, particularly in education and in health, all converged to create the impetus for sustained efforts in Washington, D.C., Beijing, Brussels, London, and a range of international capitals to better understand and deal with the country.

As the United States draws down its troop levels in Afghanistan and potentially shifts in 2015 to a train and assist mission, and the world's attention turns to newer challenges—from the civil war in Syria and the rise of the Islamic State of Iraq and as-Sham (ISIS, or Daesh, the Arabic acronym) to Russia's annexation of Crimea and the oft-mentioned pivot to East Asia—Pakistan is disappearing from the list of priorities for the international community, despite horrific, headline-grabbing violence, such as the attack on the Peshawar school children. The recent transitions in governments in the area open an opportunity to rethink approaches to the region. The combination of regional realignments and Pakistan's important internal challenges require new approaches to the region.

Why Is Pakistan a Priority?

This Working Group, a diverse collection of Pakistanis and internationals, was convened to rethink and reexamine international policies toward Pakistan at a time when critical sectors within the country are expressing a frank desire for internal reform. The world may face more pressing security challenges, but no country or region represents as potent a combination of complex security challenges, in addition to long-term economic and political opportunities, as do Pakistan and the broader South Asia region.

It is the considered opinion of The Century Foundation International Working Group on Pakistan that Pakistan's people and elites need to wake up to the dangerous reality that they face and seize the multiple opportunities that Pakistan has before it, even if doing so contradicts dogma and slogans that have substituted for serious leadership and governance. Pakistan's challenges must continue to be treated as a priority by the international community, and must be addressed squarely by Pakistan's government as well.

The consensus among Pakistan's immediate neighbors, its close allies and friends, and other countries with whom it has complicated relationships, is that a stable and secure Pakistan, capable of dealing with its internal economic, social, political, and security challenges is good for the region and good for the world. It is an absolute prerequisite for regional stability and the mitigation of potentially far-flung risks. However, the fecklessness of Pakistan's leadership makes such an outcome unlikely; the region must prepare to contain the fallout of Pakistan's continued decline. Pakistanis should wake up to the challenge and prove them wrong.

Long-complicated geopolitical and regional dynamics have accelerated in the last decade. There is little disagreement within the international community on the need for stability and security in Pakistan. This is not a matter of pure benevolence toward Pakistan, but a simple case of the broader collective interests of the international community and the specific national self-interests of the countries of which it is composed. In the words of Council on Foreign Relations senior fellow Daniel Markey, "a country of 180 million people [now 200 million], likely to be 300 million by mid-century, that borders India, China, Iran and the Arabian Sea will matter to the US, no matter what it did or did not do with bin Laden."[1] This also applies to the international community across the board, as much as the United States.

The necessity for internal change is real, a necessity that has only grown in the wake of widespread protests during the second half of 2014 by the Pakistan Tehrik-e-Insaf (PTI) and Pakistan Awami Tehrik (PAT) seeking the ouster of Prime Minister Nawaz Sharif. The protests drew upon widespread grievances about a self-serving political class and a cost-of-living crisis hitting the lower and middle classes. Critics of the protest movements argued that they deliberately weakened the authority of the civilian administration and reinforced military control over foreign and national security policy. From either perspective, the country's civilian elites have been profoundly challenged. Pakistan's ability to govern effectively and grow its economy has been hampered by the unwillingness of political elites to correct long-standing under-taxation and fiscal imbalances, institute a democratic culture that extends beyond the holding of elections on a fixed schedule, or provide protection to religious and ethnic minorities. Pakistan's complicated relationship with a wide spectrum of extremist groups is another oft-cited grievance, especially in the wake of the Peshawar attack, which saw a mobilization of civil society protests against the policies that have bred violence against Pakistanis themselves. Unless such shortcomings are addressed directly, populist calls for revolutionary change from the bottom up will only become more resonant.

Pakistani Viewpoints

There are two overriding considerations in Pakistan's dealings with the rest of the world. They are held to varying degrees by the military and InterServices Intelligence (ISI), as well as by Pakistan's diplomats. The first is national security, specifically the existential threats, real and

Figure 1.1:   *Year-to-Year Growth Rates of Per Capita GDP for South Asia,*
2001–13

Percent

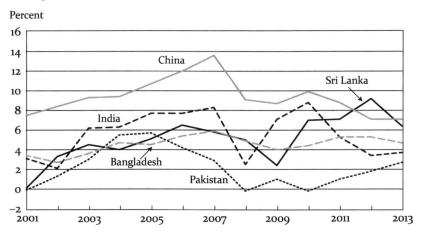

Source: "GDP per capita growth (annual %)," The World Bank, http://data.worldbank.org/indicator/
NY.GDP.PCAP.KD.ZG, accessed April 9, 2015.

perceived, from India, Afghanistan, and in the past decade, the range of
violent non-state actors that have attacked Pakistani civilian and military targets. This includes members of the newly formed al Qaeda in
the Indian Subcontinent, individuals tied to ISIS, al Qaeda-linked terror
groups such as the Tehrik-i-Taliban Pakistan, and those associated with
separatists in Balochistan.

The second consideration is the economy. More specifically, without
sustained growth of Pakistan's economy, all other policy targets (including
those of foreign policy) will over time become unattainable. The previous
decade witnessed high rates of economic growth in developing countries
generally and South Asian countries in particular (see Figure 1.1). Pakistan
has become the outlier in this pattern. Between 2001 and 2013, while per
capita income in India and Sri Lanka doubled and increased by 75 percent
in Bangladesh, it grew only by 32 percent in Pakistan.

These differences were much smaller when countries in the region
were growing slowly. But as growth has picked up, the gap between fast-
growing and slow-growing countries has expanded dramatically. If this
trend continues to the middle of this century, the per capita incomes in
India, Sri Lanka, and Bangladesh will increase by multiples of 7, 6, and
5 respectively, while in Pakistan it will only double. In other words, at

current trends, by mid-century, the residents of the rest of South Asia will be between two and three times richer than Pakistanis, on average. Stated differently, by 2050, India will have a per capita GDP of $11,000 (roughly the 2013 income level of Russia), Sri Lanka would reach $20,000 (the level of Portugal), and Bangladesh would reach that of Indonesia ($3,500); meanwhile, Pakistan would reach the current level of Honduras ($2,300). Extended another quarter century, by 2075, these trends would see India reaching a per capita income of $44,000, Bangladesh $10,000, Sri Lanka $73,000, and Pakistan $4,800. This is not to argue that these trends will necessarily continue unabated, but rather that it has now become urgent for slower growing countries, such as Pakistan, to make a big push so as to not get left behind in the region. As noted by the Nobel Laureate Paul Krugman, "productivity isn't everything but in the long run it is nearly everything."[2]

It is in the instances where there is overlap between these two overriding considerations—national security and economics—that we find Pakistan's most important foreign relationships. And it is here where the subordination of normal diplomatic and economic relations to security considerations explains the agonizingly slow speed of change in Pakistan's perceptions of India—from a security adversary to a trade partner. It also reflects the deeply complex partnership Pakistan has with the United States, the stress-laden relationship with Afghanistan, the complicated relationships with countries such as Saudi Arabia and neighboring Iran, and the longstanding ties with China, Pakistan's "all-weather" friend.

A Focus on Security

For Pakistan, security on every level is an essential problem. From its painful inception, Pakistan has lived with a fear and resentment of India that have overridden every other consideration and helped to shape the nature of state and society. Unsuccessful wars, the lack of a resolution to the question of Kashmir, and nuclear rivalry have sapped resources and strangled economic and political development in a country that has the capacity and capability to advance much further and faster. The challenge has been complicated now by the fact that the slowdown of economic growth in Pakistan will make it extremely difficult to make significant progress even toward a number of the overriding security objectives. Pakistan's leaders have sacrificed making the country into what it could be—a stable economy lifting its people out of extreme poverty—in favor of pursuing illusory and ultimately self-defeating efforts to project Pakistan as a power on a par with India.

Pakistan's relationship to Afghanistan is no less complicated, and has been—and continues to be—dominated by a security focus. One of the most striking changes in Pakistan in recent months has been its response to the new Afghan president, Ashraf Ghani, and his efforts to rescue the relationship from the dead end of undeclared hostilities. President Ghani has worked assiduously, at great risk to his domestic political standing, to establish a degree of trust with the Pakistani civilian and military leadership. To overcome the burden of history in the relationship will take sustained effort. Afghanistan was the only nation to vote against Pakistan's entry into the United Nations; its governments—even those that have been the most dependent on Pakistan, such as the Taliban—have consistently refused to accept the Durand Line as the international boundary between the two states.

Pakistan's innate sense of insecurity and its frustration at its inability to achieve its ideological objectives—"liberation" of Kashmir and parity with India—are only aggravated by the ongoing problems of Afghanistan. These include Afghan Taliban groups using (and being used by) Pakistan, millions of Afghan refugees in Pakistan, and an ongoing Pakistani Taliban insurgency in the tribal areas that threatens to spread nationwide and has brought Pakistan to the brink of civil war. Over 50,000 people have been killed in extremist-linked violence since 2003. Pakistan claims to have lost roughly twice as many soldiers as the United States in the fighting against the Taliban.[3] The vicious attack on the Army Public School in Peshawar shocked and horrified a population growing inured to Taliban violence. The apparent willingness of Pakistan's Punjabi-dominated governments to tolerate decades of discrimination and even violence against Pashtuns has further deepened ethnic rifts that threaten national unity.

The ambiguous nature of Pakistan's vision of itself, primarily colored by these fears, has led it far from the initial ideas of Jinnah—a Muslim-majority state where all citizens are equal and in which their welfare is the state's primary responsibility. The increasing dominance of the "Pakistan ideology"—defining the state's role as an unending ideological mission removed from Jinnah's vision—has encouraged sectarian attacks, most notably on minorities, including Shi'a, Christians, Hindus, Sikhs, and Ahmadis. These attacks are reflective of the gradual encroachment of activist and often violent Islamic fundamentalism on the public space and discourse of a society that had been much more tolerant in the past. It is a change in the concept of Pakistan as a home for Muslims to one of Pakistan as an activist Muslim state.[4] As Pakistan becomes more identified as a defender and champion of Sunni Islam, the status of its own minorities becomes more threatened. And as Sunni Islam becomes ever more dominated by militant versions of Deobandi and Salafi doctrines, Sunni sects such as Barelvis and Sufis—to which most of the Pakistani population adhered for centuries—have also become targets. An increasing number of anti-Shi'a attacks take place in Khyber Pakhtunkhwa, Balochistan, Karachi, and Gilgit-Baltistan with seeming impunity. The Ahmadi sect, whose adherents identify themselves as Muslims, stands marked for further discrimination and violence. Since 1974, declaring Ahmadis to be non-Muslims has constituted an unchallenged political norm in Pakistan.[5]

Women have also seen their position in society diminished by religious extremists, and there are signs that gender-based violence against women is on the increase.[6] Public opinion has changed, and the space to challenge widely held orthodoxies about religion in Pakistan has almost completely evaporated. This process has been directed by the religious right wing, with active and sustained support from mainstream political groups and the endorsement of state policy. Few are willing to speak out against extremism and in favor of a diverse and pluralist society. Some of those who have, such as Governor Salmaan Taseer of Punjab, have paid for that with their lives. Most worryingly, the future looks no brighter than the present on this front. A British Council report in 2013 surveying young people reported that 94 percent said the country was headed in the wrong direction.[7] In that survey, 38 percent favored sharia, 32 percent military rule and 29 percent democracy.

Radicalized individuals going abroad to fight and returning from fighting in foreign struggles are a part of the equation, both domestically and globally. UK officials claim a large percentage of their counterterrorism activities are related to Pakistan. There are seemingly growing links between the militants who have founded ISIS and militant groups operating in Pakistan. Senior figures in ISIS have spent time in Pakistan and Afghanistan, and TTP fighters and Waziristan-based foreign militants have both travelled to Syria and Iraq to fight, and some have formally joined ISIS. Supporters of ISIS have distributed propaganda and begun to recruit in northern Pakistan. Pakistan-based militants entertain hopes that ISIS will be prepared to fund them, a development that carries the risk of ISIS affiliates emerging as a more radical alternative to the TTP, al Qaeda and the Afghan Taliban. Some TTP commanders have already pledged loyalty to ISIS.[8] The leadership of the Red Mosque's Jamia Hafsa Madrasa, located in the very heart of Islamabad, declared its allegiance to ISIS in a video.[9] U.S. officials have contended that members of the Khorasan Group, an al Qaeda–linked organization in Syria, have also benefited from a reverse migration of militants from North Waziristan to Arab states, including a contingent of Pakistanis. Previous crises, like the aborted Time Square attack in New York in 2010 and other U.S.-related terrorism activities have had strong negative repercussions in both public opinion and among Washington officials, especially with the assumption that Pakistan either aids or abets terrorism. Militants trained in Pakistan have turned up in Somalia with al-Shabab and with various groups in Chechnya and Dagestan.

Fears of militancy emanating from Pakistan have become a source of high-level concern in China, straining its continuing and close relation-ship with Pakistan.[10] Many of the several hundred Chinese (Uighur Mus-lim) citizens reported to be fighting with ISIS in Syria and Iraq traveled through Pakistan.

In the aftermath of the Peshawar attack, it is easy to forget the long-held positions of the two principal political parties in power in Pakistan on talking to terrorists, not as a parallel track with military and intel-ligence efforts to defeat them, but as a substitute for using the force of the state to defend the population against militant extremism. Both the Pakistan Muslim League (N) and the Pakistan Tehreek-e-Insaf strongly supported and pursued accommodative dialogue with the TTP. The post-election debate over these talks with the TTP was the most vis-ible iteration of this policy. An outgrowth of a decade of conflict on the Afghanistan-Pakistan border, the TTP has no coherent political agenda or leadership, is inherently committed to anti-state violence and crim-inal activities, and benefits from significant freedom of movement on the Afghan side of the border, where Afghan Taliban and other fighters based in Pakistan have kept the Afghan government at bay. The govern-ment call for discussion with the TTP, while abandoning the fight against them, was widely regarded as a last effort to achieve some compromise with a group publicly committed to the overthrow of the Pakistani state, but without a credible political vision for Pakistan. In the end, the TTP's unwillingness or inability to abide by temporary commitments doomed even the tentative structure of talks.

After an attack by militants on Karachi's airport, on June 15, 2014, the Pakistan army launched a major military operation—Zarb e Azb, or "Sharp and Cutting Strike"—against militants in the North Waziristan Agency, thus marking the end of the government's attempts to pursue peace talks with the TTP. Until the launch of the operation, Pakistani, Afghan, and international militants had enjoyed a free run of the agency's two main towns, Mir Ali and Miranshah, and had taken full benefit of these towns' relatively developed communications and commercial infrastructure. Military leaders alleged before the offensive they had 165,000 troops in the region pitted against 20,000 terrorists, but the prospect of an all-out war and the possibilities for far-flung retaliation was something that gave Pakistanis serious cause for concern. Pashtuns noted that it was only after the militants struck outside Khyber Pakthunkwa and the Federally Administered Tribal Areas (FATA) that the Pakistani Army responded. In keeping with the pattern now established for operations in the tribal areas, the military ordered a complete evacuation of the civilian population, leading to the displacement of some 800,000 North Waziristan residents to surrounding Pakistani districts and even Khost and Paktika provinces in Afghanistan. This mass displacement of Pashtuns to areas where the Pakistan authorities are reluctant to grant aid agencies full access continues to pose a major humanitarian challenge and to exacerbate ethnic tensions.

The outcome of the military operation has been mixed at best. The army was successful in regaining control of two main population centers, Miranshah and Mir Ali, and effectively excluding all militants from them. In the process, the army inflicted massive and widespread damage on the civilian infrastructure, despite facing little resistance from the militants, who withdrew in the face of overwhelming force. Although the operation left TTP seriously disrupted, the capacity of anti-Afghan government groups such as the Haqqani Network to strike Kabul and surrounding areas was clearly undiminished, as such groups had simply relocated their operations to other areas of Afghanistan and Pakistan. The lasting impact on the international militant capacity in North Waziristan depends on the actions of the Pakistan Army to extend the operation into the remoter border tracts of the agency, which initially it only targeted from the air. With the apparent fissures and rivalries within the TTP, it is not clear how the threat will evolve in the near future. Nevertheless, the challenge of internal militancy promises to be a long-term problem for Pakistan. And, even if Pakistan is successful in clearing FATA of militants, such an operation could lead to further problems in the region. The rising number of internally displaced persons is but one emergent challenge. Terrorist attacks continue unabated in Khyber Pakhtunkhwa in spite of pre-electoral pledges by the Pakistan Tehreek-e-Insaf (PTI) to bring peace to the province.

Even with the mixed results of the military offensive, its initiation marks a watershed in Pakistani politics. Pakistan's mainstream parties had lined up behind the army's operation, as they have behind the controversial decision to amend the constitution and establish military courts. Such has been the impact of the Peshawar attack. The unprecedented mobilization of public opinion, however, seems to have been used so far solely for a series of vindictive measures designed to inflict pain on terrorists and their abettors in Pashtun-inhabited areas, rather than measures that will eventually help establish a more inclusive and pluralist Pakistan.

The Challenge of Economics and Governance

With the Pakistani state firmly focused on its security challenges, economic and governance concerns have taken a secondary position. The resulting "business as usual" climate has produced poor leadership, an unresponsive civilian government, and a society prone to extremism and incapable of embracing its own diversity. A reform agenda has long included a revised relationship between federal authorities and the FATA, Karachi, and Balochistan. Rationalization of the legal status of the FATA and strengthening of democratic rule over Balochistan have been recommendations for maintaining sound governance and building the capacity to deal with militant threats. Alongside these efforts must be a serious effort by Pakistan's political elites to increase the competence of the administrative apparatus of the Pakistani state, which has been starved of both funds and talent and used by governing politicians to support their own clan and family interests. Those deficiencies are repeated across the economic and education sectors: Pakistan is danger-ously underinvesting in its next generation of human capital.

These questions highlight a number of vicious as well as potentially virtuous cycles. For example, the widening of income gaps within a region has geopolitical implications, as lower-income countries find it increas-ingly difficult to defend their sovereignty. Income differences translate into widening gaps in budgetary resources, most notably resources for defense expenditures, which in turn enhance paranoia as well as genu-ine insecurity, and push countries toward more inward-oriented options, and lower growth prospects. Similarly, a lack of resources resulting in energy scarcity slows down growth, which in turn leads to further energy scarcity. Finally, as popular sentiment becomes more responsive to the potential economic benefits of regional cooperation, the backlash from entrenched interests can turn the country further inward, thus exacer-bating regional income inequalities.

The critical importance of rapid economic growth in breaking these vicious cycles has been noted in Vision 2025, Pakistan's framework for long-term socioeconomic change.[11] This framework sets out an ambitious set of targets for Pakistan's future development, most notably that of reaching high-income status by the centennial of independence in 2047. Vision 2025 also identified seven priority areas: People First, Inclusive Growth, Governance, Water/Energy/Food Security, Promoting Entrepre-neurship, the Knowledge Economy, and Regional Connectivity.

The major drivers or determinants of economic expansion are popula-tion growth, energy access, governance (in terms of both the ability to manage conflict and the capacity of the state), and international trade.

It is important to point out that a rapid decline in population growth is closely correlated with the acceleration of economic growth. Intui-tively, this pattern makes eminent sense. The reduction of population growth rates frees investment resources from having to cater predomi-nantly to the needs of a growing population (more schools, more hos-pitals, more housing) rather than to more productive investments. No country has made the transition from a low income developing status to a developed country status without a significant reduction in the popu-lation growth rate.

The rate of population growth in Pakistan, however, is second only to Nepal's in the South Asian region. At 1.84 percent per year, it is significantly higher than Bangladesh (1.67 percent), India (1.46 percent), and Sri Lanka (0.48 percent). Sri Lanka, Maldives, Vietnam, and China were the first to lower their population growth rates among developing countries in the region, and also the first to experience high growth rates. India and Bangladesh have followed suit. Pakistan and Nepal bring up the rear. In the future, reducing population growth to spur economic growth will remain a critical challenge for Pakistan's policymakers.

On the energy front, Pakistanis are only too well aware of the enormous costs imposed by the lack of access to modern energy services. The chronic blackouts and load-shedding hinder productive capacity, lower the quality of life, exacerbate inequality, affect the environment adversely, and undermine governance as well as social services. Unfortunately, these challenges are occurring in a period when the long-term trend of domestic energy prices is upwards (notwithstanding the huge swings, both upwards and downwards, observed since 2005). Despite the repeated attempts at formulating an effective energy strategy, the situation has not improved.

The issue of governance in Pakistan, as mentioned earlier, pertains on the one hand to civic peace and on the other hand to the capacity and legitimacy of the state. The role of civic peace in promoting economic growth—and that of conflict in depressing it—is well known. The relationship works in both directions. Just as conflict leads to stagnation, stagnation exacerbates conflict. The inability of the economy to generate decent jobs in adequate numbers to absorb the growing number of young people is a sure recipe for social disruption.

The other aspect of governance that affects economic growth is the capacity of the state to maintain law and order, provide essential services, build infrastructure, and promote development. This capacity depends critically on public revenues, which have declined precipitously in Pakistan. The share of taxes in GDP has declined from about 12 percent in the early 1990s to less than 10 percent today. This is contrary to the trend in all developing countries, where the tax-to-GDP ratio increases with affluence. In India, for example, this ratio has now reached close to 20 percent, from a similar base as Pakistan in the early 1990s. Considering the fact that Pakistan allocates over 3 percent of these revenues to defense expenditures, the gap in social and development spending is even larger. It is absolutely essential for Pakistan's future growth, welfare, sovereignty, and security that the tax-to-GDP ratio be increased.

The low tax-to-GDP ratio has contributed to the multifaceted crisis of the state. Low government salaries result in rising corruption levels. Inadequate resources for police and judicial systems lead to escalating levels of crime and criminality. Inadequate resources for education mean lack of access to education, increasing inequality, low levels of skill, worsening prospects for employment, and the increasing allure of criminal activity. Inadequate resources for public health result in low quality of life and life expectancy. Inadequate resources for energy investments increase economic, social, and environmental costs.

In the absence of adequate tax revenues, the gap has been filled partially by international economic assistance. Such assistance provides a steady stream of grants and loans that help prop up the inadequate and dysfunctional fiscal and economic system of Pakistan. It also compensates for the inability of the economy to earn foreign resources through exports of goods and services. This pursuit of economic assistance is not a secondary element of what Pakistan demands. It has been and remains central to all of Pakistan's relations.

In more recent years, there has been an effort to scale back the narrative from efforts to generate aid, and to focus more clearly on trade, as a driver of economic stability and a remedy for the unchanged political economy of under-taxation and fiscal imbalances. While trade inflows cannot fully offset the need for aid (unless the fiscal system is reformed and made more relevant to modern demands), they do relax the foreign exchange constraint and provide the most reliable engine for growth.

Pakistan, however, has done very poorly in promoting trade. In the two decades from 1993 to 2013, Pakistan's exports increased from $8.4 billion, to $30.1 billion; that is, roughly three-and-a-half times. In the same period, Bangladesh's exports increased more than tenfold, and India's by a factor of seventeen. Within South Asia, only Nepal performed more poorly than Pakistan (see Table 1.1). As is well known, the performance of some of the East and Southeast Asian economies was even more dramatic in this regard. Chinese exports (from the mainland alone) increased by a factor of 28, and Vietnam's by a factor of 38.

If Pakistan is to witness a period of rapid growth, the conceptual framework behind "trade not aid" needs to be expanded far beyond what has previously been discussed. A trade regime solely focused on one sector (such as agriculture) is only a first step; a progressive integration of the Pakistani economy into the global economy would require a broad suite

Table 1.1: *Exports of Goods and Services from South Asian Countries, 1993 and 2013*

US$ millions, in current prices

	1993 (US$ million)	2013 (US$ million)	Increase (%)
Bangladesh	3,074	32,743	965.16
Bhutan	92	669	627.17
India	27,123	464,188	1,611.42
Maldives	213	2,745	1,188.73
Nepal	730	2,174	197.81
Pakistan	8,366	30,071	259.44
Sri Lanka	3,420	15,079	340.91
South Asia	43,018	547,669	1273.11

Source: United Nations Conference on Trade and Development, UNCTADstat database, unctadstat. unctad.org, accessed 19 January 2015.

of policy changes, including institution of supportive fiscal and monetary policies, capacity building of export industries, investing in quality enhancement and reliability, ensuring energy access for exporters, and strengthening of trade missions, especially in rapidly growing markets.

A greater Pakistani focus on trade can also provide the elements of a new national narrative regarding its relations with India. Given the speed of export growth in India, and remembering that there is a similar pattern in import growth, a logical progression would be for Pakistani goods to find a market in the Indian economy. Not only would this be a win-win scenario for both countries, it might produce positive outcomes in political and social domains.

Indeed, there is considerable interest in such positive scenarios. Trade with India and regional economic cooperation are the vehicles through which a refreshing and bold series of initiatives by Pakistani administrations across three regimes (General Pervez Musharraf, President Asif Ali Zardari, and Prime Minister Sharif) have been attempted, though those early efforts faced traditional challenges and foes.[12] More recently, Sharif's endeavors in this arena have been hobbled by the political crisis fomented by the PTI/PAT protests, leading to an apparent reassertion by the military and ISI of their total prerogatives over foreign and security policies. For its part, the administration of Prime Minister Narendra Modi and his Hindu nationalist party, the Bharatiya Janata Party (BJP) has taken a rigid approach to Pakistan that has seen an escalation of tensions along the border and the suspension of normal dialogue between the top diplomats of each country.[13] Modi's continuing acerbic attitude and statements following his protests at meetings between Pakistani diplomats and Kashmiri Muslims during his inauguration are unhelpful to the ongoing efforts on many levels to bring the two nations closer together.

The Need to Reframe U.S. and International Engagement with Pakistan

The overwhelming centrality of security as the primary driver of international interest in Pakistan imposes limitations to both the framing and the analysis of Pakistan, as well as how international capitals, particularly Washington, can engage with the country. The most important of these limitations is that the lens through which Pakistan is examined privileges the role of security—particularly the security of the United States and its allies—which elevates the Pakistani military establishment above all other factors and institutions, including the security of Pakistanis themselves.

The U.S. also needs to wake up about Pakistan. This one-sided view of Pakistan generates an imbalance in the narrative, at great cost—both to the interests of those in the international community who believe a constructive relationship is possible, and to the interests of 200 million Pakistanis, among whom only a small minority are actively invested in these dynamics. This "security above all else" approach toward Pakistan has actually exacerbated the country's metastasizing political problems, which have posed a distinct issue for the region, and are now destabilizing Pakistan itself.

The greatest victim of this disequilibrium has been Pakistan's democratic institutions. Every explicit military intervention in Pakistani politics has been accompanied by an era of economic assistance that enabled incompetent and dysfunctional military rulers dependent on the United States. Pakistan's long-term security issues and its long-standing regional relationships were never perfect, but they were systematically made worse during periods of military rule. All of Pakistan's military regimes instigated military conflict, negatively impacted human rights, and weakened civilian institutions—with disastrous ramifications for the ability of their successors to navigate complex security, economic, and governance issues. Field Marshall Ayub Khan, who rose in a coup to be Pakistan's president from 1958 to 1969, helped worsen already-fraught relations with India. Yahya Khan oversaw a bloody crackdown in what was then East Pakistan in 1971, embroiling Pakistan in another unsuccessful war with India. General Zia ul-Haq, who also seized power in a coup in 1977, not only destroyed Pakistan's hopes for a pluralistic political culture, but also did unmitigated damage to both Afghanistan and long-term relations between Pakistan and Afghanistan. (He also created the infrastructure of training that is generating terrorists and suicide bombers today.) General Musharraf was the perfect combination of both Ayub and Zia—fooling gullible Western audiences with liberal charm on the one hand, while with the other fanning the flames of violent Islamism as an instrument of national security strategy and deceiving himself and others into thinking he could control the fallout.

As this security-only approach to Pakistan has produced problematic dynamics, it holds one guarantee. Without a major course correction by nations engaging with Pakistan in the degree of importance they afford to security factors, the on-again, off-again romance between the West and the Pakistani military establishment is bound to be on-again. This reality will have fatal consequences for the strength of democratic institutions within Pakistan, regardless of whatever short-term success against terrorism it might generate.

Pakistan's civilian governments have also had their own failings, compounded by the toxic environments they have often inherited. While delivering the outward exercise of democracy, including regular elections, they have often regularly fallen short of tapping the full promise of Pakistani society, captured as they are by elite interests and the prerogatives of patronage—all the while looking over their shoulders at the military in fear of the next coup. They have not done the hard work of building institutions of governance, preferring instead to coast on the colonial institutional heritage and the strength of the military. Their attitudes have often been feudal in nature, reflecting vote-bank politics and patronage (including appointees in civilian positions based less on merit than on political connections), and support for family, clan, and tribal interests, rather than actual delivery of services to the whole of its citizenry. They have tended not to make long-term policies, partly out of fear of being ousted prematurely. Their quick endorsement of military courts is suggestive of their willingness to cede critical national security decision-making to military rather than civilian institutions, which has the effect of hollowing out—or never even building—much-needed civilian capacity.

Absent a truly robust economy and vigorous governance structure, both military leaders and civilian rulers alike view Western capitals as sources of quick, cheap, no-questions-asked bailout money. And in turn these capitals' driving fear of Pakistani insecurity, which is likely to impact them, prompts them to reciprocate, supporting and sustaining bailouts for Pakistani leaders—especially during military rule, when security factors dominate more than usual. The shame is that those who underwrite these bailouts do not adequately consider the long-term damage that they do to the organic, democratic, national conversation in Pakistan that seeks reform.

Ultimately, without a wholesale reframing of the international approach to Pakistan—and the region, itself dependent on a major recalibration of Pakistan's security posture and policy—there is little chance that the cycle will stop.

Right now, Pakistan's greatest challenges are related to the human security of its own population, the quality of its governance, the vitality and robustness of its economy, and the degree to which Pakistan's next generation is being prepared and cared for—from their nutrition and health to their education and future economic opportunities. Enduring engagement between the international community and Islamabad on these key issues will not happen as long as they continue to be supplanted by concerns with military and state security—a short-term approach that only privileges issues such as nuclear weapons development, terrorism, and Afghanistan's instability. A relationship defined by financial support in exchange for security measures, with no other impetus for broader reform, is neither in Pakistan's long-term interest, nor in that of the countries and institutions that may provide such support.

The change in approach being advocated is made imperative by a realistic appraisal of interests. Pakistan has a greater potential to be a market for global products and services than the current flow of capital and trade suggests. Few countries have 200 million consumers, and even fewer of them have a population growing younger, with currently over 100 million Pakistanis below the age of twenty-five. While this huge potential market underscores the opportunities in Pakistan, it also marks the need for immediate policy changes: a high rate of population growth makes it extremely difficult for rapid economic growth to take place.

Pakistan offers the quickest and potentially cheapest conduit for trade between the Middle East and China, between Africa and China, and between Afghanistan and the world. Pakistan's energy needs today, and over the course of the next quarter–century, are likely to remain unmet solely by domestic supply, which creates opportunities for energy surplus countries among the Central Asian states and Middle Eastern suppliers. Iran, for example, has in the past offered to help build natural gas infrastructure to Pakistan, to which the United States has objected. Recent press reports suggest that China is willing to finance the construction of Pakistan's portion of the pipeline. Such a breakthrough based primarily on improving U.S.-Iran relations has the potential to ameliorate Iranian-Pakistani ties, in turn reducing Sunni/Shi'a tensions, as well as lessening tensions in Balochistan. This could be an early, positive reaction to an Iranian nuclear agreement.

Pakistan's potential role as a serious economic actor in the region could be instrumental to a range of other countries' economic plans as well. The last decade has seen a proliferation of multilateral conceptions of the region as a fully integrated trading hub. These include: CASA 1000, an electricity transmission project linking Central and South Asia; the Tajikistan-Afghanistan-Pakistan-India natural gas pipeline; the Iran-Pakistan-India natural gas pipeline; the Chinese "Silk Road Economic Belt," and a separate but related economic corridor linking China and Pakistan; and the American "New Silk Road," a similar effort for integrating Afghanistan into regional trade flows. While these infrastructure projects are of varying feasibility and would be years in the making they speak to a conception of the region significantly more connected than currently. Recently, the China-Pakistan economic corridor has received renewed attention as President Xi Jinping has made it a priority in China's relationship with Pakistan. During President Xi's April 2015 state visit to Pakistan, China signed agreements totalling $28 billion out of a proposed $46 billion package of investments. However, fears of the impact of anti-Chinese Islamic militancy disrupting the plans persist. The project is also narrowly conceived as linking China to Pakistan through Pakistani-administered Kashmir. Its full potential rests on expanding the infrastructure investments to include connections to Afghanistan and India.[14]

Greater economic engagement with China seems a logical step for a host of reasons. Pakistan sees China as its only trusted ally. Official relations between the two countries are excellent and many Pakistanis see China as a foreign policy alternative to the United States, especially after the United States improved its cooperation over nuclear issues with India (China, however, does not completely share this view and consistently advises Pakistan to repair its relations with the United States). In turn, China has proposed a $46 billion program for investment in Pakistan, including a refinery at the port of Gwadar on the Indian Ocean, which it now manages. There are discussions to build oil and gas pipelines through Pakistan along the Karakoram highway to western China. Pakistan is the largest purchaser of Chinese weapons, taking 47 percent of its export market. Recently Pakistan's government approved a $4-5 billion purchase of eight submarines.[15] Chinese-Pakistani cooperation has extended to military training and operations, as well as to nuclear development. Chinese engagement in Pakistan has not yet involved outright aid, but as China becomes increasingly involved in the region, this may change. China has held back from getting involved in the Indo-Pakistan strategic rivalries. China wants to be friends with both Pakistan and India, not least because of a booming $60 billion in trade ties with India, as opposed to only $9 billion with Pakistan. More importantly, while the world has focused on the dramatic increase in Chinese exports (twenty-eight-fold between 1993 and 2013), what has often been ignored is that China's imports have risen at the same (and often higher) speeds. Indeed, China adds more to global aggregate demand every year than any other country in the world. Pakistan is in a strong position to gain entry into the fastest growing import market in the world. China is a logical partner for Pakistan in the modernization of its infrastructure; likewise, Pakistan could also use western China as a logistical corridor for connecting to Central Asia.

Building these connections will take decades, but the foundations for this vision must be laid now.

What Do Pakistanis Want?

The manner in which one defines the Pakistani state informs how to assess its self-perception and thus its interests. Pakistan's elite are not a monolith. The military is one obvious stakeholder, particularly given its continued close control of Pakistan's foreign and national security policy. After the Peshawar attack, it is clear that the power of the military will grow, both informally, as it becomes involved in provincial governance through provincial apex committees, and formally, through the military courts established through the Twenty-First Amendment to the constitution.[16]

Politicians and elected leaders that work through the formal democratic institutions of Pakistan, however, will continue to be extremely important stakeholders, perhaps even more so after Peshawar, as the need for better civil-military relations grow in significance. Among the most important elements of the Pakistani state is the formal bureaucracy, the various ministries at the federal and provincial level, which are vital to the pursuit of public policy for both politicians and the generals that run the military. While in many areas the civil-military divide has been bridged dramatically in the past decade, it is easy to overestimate the impact of that progress.

The conduct of foreign policy as well as the actions of the state domestically have often been said to be at odds with the aspirations of the Pakistani people, a result to be expected of a country that has both multifarious geopolitical challenges and a history of non-democratic, authoritarian decision-making. These factors have conspired to make Pakistan's foreign policy challenges all the more complex.

One measure of this complexity is the manner in which Pakistanis perceive the international community. In a 2013 Pew Survey, Pakistanis had the highest differential among all nations between those with a favorable view of the United States and favorable views of China.[17] Bilateral relations between the United States and Pakistan face this significant complication and have to overcome mainstream sentiments working against that relationship. Any reasonable analysis must treat the distrust of the United States within the Pakistani mainstream with an honest and fair assessment, much as it should recognize whatever implications exist of the enormous goodwill China enjoys in the country.

The best way to dissect what Pakistanis want in terms of relations with the rest of the world is to assess the choices Pakistanis made in the 2008 and 2013 elections. In both elections, Pakistanis chose center-left and center-right parties (the PPP in 2008 and the PML-N in 2013), forswearing rabidly anti-American, right-wing groups. Both elections produced governments with overtly pro-peace and pro-normalization policies with India. Both elections produced a leadership that, at least rhetorically, was committed to supporting and strengthening Afghanistan in its quest for security, stability, and peace. Both elections produced governments willing to work with the United States to varying degrees.

Of course, it is important to see these electoral choices in their proper context. The popular vote in Pakistan, particularly in 2013, included a clear expression of the willingness to engage terrorist groups like the TTP in dialogue rather than to conduct full-scale military operations against them, a perspective that slowly changed among some elite sectors. The popular vote also seemed to express a desire to hold the United States to account for actions that are broadly perceived as violations of Pakistani autonomy and sovereignty—such as U.S. drone strikes on Pakistani soil. The emergence of the PTI as a major political force exposed for the first time a growing urbanization of the political discourse, in which middle class rage, especially anti-American rage, increasingly defines the Pakistani center.

So how should the various impulses of the Pakistani people be interpreted? Most Pakistanis want some version of the ideal Pakistan as informed by the versions of history that the state has articulated throughout the past forty years. Pakistanis are also impatient for change. Much of the youth population is growing disillusioned with current political elites and the inability of elections alone to deliver better government. Islam is central to the identity of many Pakistanis at the individual, community, and institutional level. Justice is an overriding theme in the public discourse and the ambiguous linkages between religion and an administrative system that can deliver justice are possibly the single greatest source of fuel for the radical right wing and its quest for relevance in Pakistan. The heretofore limited political role of the right wing is as important as its potency in shifting the national conversation, constructing rigid boundaries, stigmatizing and intimidating dissenting voices, and preventing reform.

Increasingly, the hopes of Pakistan being true to the organic diversity of the people that have inhabited the area that makes up the country are under threat at the hands of those who reject pluralism and are unwilling to allow it to grow. Attacks on liberals, both rhetorically and through physical violence, are on the rise. This is an unhappy portent for those that claim to be for Muhammad Ali Jinnah's Pakistan, a country that is a homeland for the Subcontinent's Muslims, but whose government is officially secular and inclusive of all faiths.[18]

There is no average Pakistani given the wide geographic and cultural diversity of the country—but the pulse of Pakistan can be taken from the mix of indicators that shape the discourse. Chief among them is the mass media, and the choices Pakistanis make in news and entertainment. Pakistanis consume a wide variety of viewpoints on evening television talk shows. They cannot stop packing the cinema halls for Bollywood productions while simultaneously sympathizing with militants who claim to work for a free Kashmir. They react viscerally, and often violently, to anything perceived as anti-Islam. Declining freedom of operation for Pakistani press outlets has become particularly pronounced, with charges of blasphemy brought against reporters from several media organizations, though this duality is visible throughout the discourse and across issues.

In this way, Pakistan is very much like any large country with a vibrant national discourse. The uniqueness of Pakistan lies not here, but in the specific kinds of threats Pakistani society and state face and the set of failures that those threats are exacerbating.

CHAPTER TWO

Managing Key Regional Security Challenges

Pakistan's relations with its neighbors are among the central challenges facing it; concerns about security and stability animate the international community's discussions about and policy in the region. In particular, the future of the Afghan-Pakistan and India-Pakistan bilateral relationships are essential to unlocking the region's full potential. To date, progress toward that end has been hampered by concerns of transnational terrorism and nuclear weapons development. Building on progress that has been achieved in relations with Afghanistan recently and restarting a process of normalization between India and Pakistan must be near-term goals for both the international community and the respective states.

Afghanistan

Afghanistan will continue to be a security issue for Pakistan for the foreseeable future. Primary among the complexities is the presence on both sides of the border of a large Pashtun population, two-thirds of which is in Pakistan. Taliban groups, mainly but not solely Pashtun, as well as other militant groups of various nationalities, use both sides of the border as safe havens. The departure of most of the international military forces from Afghanistan in 2014 may aggravate the situation, but also provides an opening to reset the relationship. In the past, Pakistan's desire to have a friendly regime in Kabul has led it to engage in aggressive activities to help bring this about, including support for the Afghan Taliban and the Haqqani Network. The recent efforts by both Pakistan's civilian and military leadership to support the recognized government in Kabul have ameliorated the environment, as evidenced by the positive meetings during President Ashraf Ghani's trip to Pakistan in November 2014 and the improvement in relations since. At the same time, Afghanistan's friendship with India—one of the ten largest donors to Afghanistan—triggers Islamabad's basic insecurities. Indian activities such as building a trade route from the Iranian port of Chabahar and setting up its first foreign military base in Tajikistan only aggravate Pakistani concerns. The new unity government in Kabul offers an unprecedented opportunity for the two nations to put relations on a long-range path where the needs of both countries are considered.

Pakistan and Afghanistan's difficult relationship will continue to impact the economic and political developments in both countries. Even if talks in Pakistan with the Pakistani Taliban had led to changes in the governance of FATA and Khyber Pakhtunkhwa, the problem for Afghanistan of safe harbor for Afghan Taliban on the Pakistani side of the border would remain; likewise, growing safe havens for the TTP in Kunar and Nuristan provinces of Afghanistan are now a critical security concern of Pakistan.

Afghanistan's refusal to accept the border officially is one impediment to the relationship, but the impracticality of regulating the border except along major roads is a more important obstacle. The new Ghani government will have the opportunity to place relations on a better plane, while the withdrawal of most foreign forces from Afghanistan in 2014 opens the door to new possibilities. In the worst case, a civil war could break out again in Afghanistan and there could be a gradual dissolution of the government set up in Afghanistan after 2001 with the reassertion of authority by provincial power brokers, a situation which has never entirely disappeared. Pakistan needs to guide carefully its relationship with Afghanistan, especially in times of internal conflict and continue to be aware that Taliban groups are focused on both sides of the border.

Since the inauguration of President Ghani, the atmosphere between Afghanistan and Pakistan has changed remarkably quickly. Ghani's state visit to Beijing, the first of his presidency, ratified China's emergence as an important force in the international effort to stabilize Afghanistan, a role that is welcomed by Pakistan, Afghanistan, and the United States. Ghani then addressed the Beijing ministerial meeting of the Istanbul/Heart of Asia Process, which China has chaired for over a year, and where Pakistan agreed to take the chair for the coming year. Pakistan and China thus confirmed the legitimacy of a regional platform centered on Afghanistan and including India, Iran, and Russia. Pakistan is likely to hand off the chairmanship to India in a year, which will require unprecedented cooperation between the two countries. Afghanistan, Pakistan, and the United States supported a Chinese proposal to establish a Regional Forum for Afghan Reconciliation centered in Beijing within the framework of the Heart of Asia Process. Though Russia postponed its official adoption, these states are likely to proceed. Pakistan would not have accepted the chair of the Heart of Asia Process if it foresaw a coming year of destabilization in Afghanistan—it will therefore feel pressure to make its chairmanship a success.

The two countries further established the basis for that success during President Ghani's official visit to Islamabad, where he met both the president and the army chief of staff, General Raheel Sharif. The two sides agreed on an unprecedented agenda of economic cooperation and integration, including the doubling of trade within two years and the establishment of preferential zones for Pakistani investment in several regions of Afghanistan. The two countries agreed on very significant measures of security cooperation and border management. More quietly, they agreed that during the coming winter they would work together to put a peace process in place so that this spring will see a peace offensive rather than a war offensive.

The two governments have quickly established a framework beyond what we would have dared to recommend only a few months ago. Our recommendation now is for Pakistan to bear in mind the very deep skepticism of Afghan public opinion about any policies of Islamabad and to implement quickly visible confidence building measures with concrete benefits. Consistent clarity of intentions should be the hallmark of diplomatic efforts going forward. One indicator of the growing comfort level between Islamabad and Kabul was the immediate visit of General Sharif to Afghanistan following the Peshawar attack. Both sides gave the outward appearance of a joint resolve to fight terror rather than descending into mutual recriminations about state sponsorship of terrorism. Subsequent to that visit, Afghanistan arrested five TTP members found on its soil.[1]

Over the coming months, Pakistan and Afghanistan must coordinate messaging to the Afghan Taliban to let them know that: (1) Pakistan will not support, facilitate, or tolerate violence against the Afghan government and people, but will support efforts to enable the Taliban to return to Afghanistan with security and dignity; and (2) Afghanistan will cooperate with Pakistan to frustrate the use of violence, but will engage with the Taliban seriously to resolve the obstacles to Afghanistan becoming the common home of all Afghans. Coordinated support from the United States and China will help make these assurances credible for all concerned. Both countries should consider whether a mediator from the United Nations or another institution could assist the process, as recommended in The Century Foundation's previous Task Force report on Afghanistan.[2]

The unprecedented thaw in relations between Afghanistan and Pakistan that followed President Ashraf Ghani's November 2014 visit to Islamabad presents the region with the best prospect for peace and stability in decades. The assistance of China in the reconciliation process both between the neighboring states and with the Afghan Taliban is also a new and very positive factor. President Ghani's politically costly gestures to build confidence in Pakistan through security and intelligence cooperation, suspending a weapons deal with India, making detailed plans for cooperative border management, and providing access to Pakistani investors require full and even asymmetrical reciprocation from Pakistan to assure that he has concrete gains to show a skeptical population that cooperation with Pakistan is fruitful.

So far, Pakistan seems to be making an unprecedented serious effort to press the Afghan Taliban, including its leader, Mullah Muhammad Omar, to join talks with the Kabul government. If the Taliban agree, Pakistan must do its best to assure that they negotiate seriously, above all by removing the Taliban's military option in Afghanistan. Every spring the Taliban infiltrate thousands of fighters from Pakistan into Afghanistan and announce an offensive. It is imperative that this year Pakistan cooperate fully with the Afghan security forces to blunt that offensive in order to send a clear message that the Taliban no longer have the option to refuse negotiation while waiting unmolested in their Pakistani sanctuary. The results will provide tremendous benefit to both countries.

To realize the trade-related aspects of the agenda would be the logical next-step, cementing an improving political and security relationship with an economic one. A modernized and competent, honest, border and customs apparatus could bring in vitally needed additional income to both governments, as well as opening Pakistan for trans-shipment from India. For this, trust between India and Pakistan needs to improve significantly.

The granting of Most Favored Nation status to India by Pakistan could be one step in the right direction; the lowering of non-tariff barriers on the Indian side could be a symmetrical commitment to moving the overall relationship forward. There are still upwards of two million Afghans in Pakistan, documented and not, most of them born and raised there but still Afghan citizens. They often have ties on both sides of the border and engage in cross-border trade, legal and illegal. Pakistani financial support for these refugees, partially reimbursed by United Nations High Commission for Refugees (UNHCR), is a burden on the Pakistani government, which has been working with the government of Afghanistan to repatriate them. An outbreak of civil war in Afghanistan would undoubtedly lead to another outflow of refugees into western Pakistan, exacerbating the tension already extant there.

Both Pakistan and Afghanistan have the potential to serve as trade corridors to Central Asia and westward on to Europe.[3] The New Silk Road project and others envision a network of highways and railroads linking Eurasia. The logic is there. However, the will to proceed is lacking. In a peaceful situation, a truck could move from Tashkent in Uzbekistan to Karachi in less than two days. As Russia and China work to line up Central Asian countries in their own economic spheres, Pakistan partnering with Afghanistan could provide a healthy alternative to big neighbor domination. The Casa-1000 project, linking transmission lines to sell surplus electricity from Tajikistan and Kyrgyzstan to Afghanistan and Pakistan, is a further example of what could be done.

Pakistan should use its influence in Afghanistan to shore up its democracy and encourage democratic inclusiveness rather than support specific ethnic groups and encouraging an Afghanistan that is unstable and thus by definition a problem for Pakistan.

India: Challenges to and Opportunities for Normalization

While the willingness of the Pakistani political elite to engage in a normalization process is oft-expressed, the process has been stalled since the return to civilian rule in 2008 and the Mumbai terrorist attacks that same year. The indications from Islamabad are that normalization enjoys a wide consensus among Pakistani civilian elites. The pro-peace lobby is, however, vulnerable to two factors—one internal to Pakistan, another having to do with domestic Indian realities.

The first factor is the machinations of a domestic anti-peace lobby with links to potent terrorist groups. As previously referenced, a constellation of Islamist militant groups operate within Pakistan's borders. Some are dedicated to specifically anti-Shi'a violence, while others, most famously Lashkar-e-Taiba (LeT), are dedicated to countering the Indian government through terrorist violence, especially in Kashmir. The alleged links between these groups and the Pakistani military-intelligence apparatus creates a nexus whereby the security establishment's "veto" over key foreign policy issues such as relations with India is backed up on the ground by acts of terrorism designed to derail any forward progress. Civilian accountability is nonexistent for these elements of Pakistan's national security strategy, a fact that further complicates any concerted action against extremism country-wide.

The second is the reception that peace overtures and efforts on the Pakistani side are met with in New Delhi and across the Indian political and security establishment, particularly in the face of seeming impunity enjoyed by anti-Indian militants based in Pakistan. The Indian government has been quite forthright in demanding more action by Pakistan against anti-Indian extremist groups, especially the LeT. The lack of progress on Pakistani legal proceedings against LeT members linked to the Mumbai attacks is a particular source of contention. The initial rhetoric of the Modi government has been much more strident even with its public outreach after events like Peshawar. Allowing bail for alleged Mumbai mastermind Zaki-ur-Rehman Lakhvi was but one development that was difficult to understand in India.

Despite current issues, Prime Ministers Sharif and Modi could eventually develop a working relationship to advance normalization. There is certainly a precedent in Sharif's relationship with the previous Bharatiya Janata Party-affiliated prime minister, Atal Bihari Vajpayee. In those circumstances, it was the Pakistani military that played the role of spoiler, inciting a conflict over Kargil that decisively set back the Lahore process. While Modi's history as chief minister of Gujarat, in particular during the 2002 communal riots there, as well as his Rashtriya Swayamsevak Sangh and Hindutva-preaching allies, may militate against an agenda of reaching out to Pakistan, he may accept the need for change and moderate the longer he is in office. This outcome may be determined in large part by the necessity of the new Indian government to accelerate economic growth through expanded trade. While campaigning in India's Lok Sabha elections, Modi suggested that both nations faced the challenge of overcoming crippling poverty and that India was ready to work with Pakistan if the Pakistanis could end the de facto safe havens for anti-Indian militants.[4] At the same time, Modi has taken a hard-line rhetorical stance over militant infiltration into Kashmir and recent armed clashes across the Line of Control.[5] A new round of tensions grew out of the Modi government's protests and subsequent cancellation of bilateral talks over a meeting between Pakistan's High Commissioner and the Hurriyat Conference, a coalition of Kashmiri separatist leaders, despite the fact that such meetings had been cause for only mild protests in the past.

It is also critical that discussion of normalization reach beyond the oft-expressed and fitfully implemented desire to improve trade relations. Confidence-building at the strategic level should be pursued in tandem with more opportunities for progress on non-governmental fronts. More people-to-people exchanges would be one place to start. Additionally, given that India and Pakistan face common economic and human development challenges (poverty, infant mortality, health and hygiene, and female empowerment), there is an opportunity for collaboration and sharing of best-practices in social welfare and protection programs.

What is clear is that a continuation of the status quo will continue to diminish both sides and set back the region. The international community should recognize the importance of a durable India-Pakistan relationship as an enabling condition for stability in Afghanistan. The opportunity cost of the current stasis on trade and strategic relations is too high not to be addressed promptly, particularly for Pakistan. According to research from the New America Foundation, the trade potential between the two nations is ten times higher than current levels due to a combination of physical and regulatory barriers.[6] Whichever approach and nomenclature is ultimately accepted, Most Favored Nations or non-discriminatory Market Access, it needs to be the centerpiece of post-2015 thinking about the bilateral relationship and approaches to the region as a whole. An increase in investment and harmonization of regulatory regimes—from visas to foreign direct investment to strengthening the border infrastructure—will be necessary. Both sides should work to return to normal diplomatic discussions to de-escalate and prevent armed clashes along the Line of Control, while pursuing other avenues for confidence-building at both the governmental and popular level.

Yemen and Potential Spillover Effects

Pakistan's relations with key allies and neighbors now face an additional and perhaps unwanted complication in light of Saudi Arabia's recent request for Pakistani support of its military offensive against Houthi rebels in Yemen in the form of aircraft, warships, and soldiers. The request came at a time of increased sectarian polarization and proxy conflict in the Middle East and beyond. Many Sunni Arab states allege that the Houthis, a rebel movement led by Zaydi Shi'a, represent the latest Iranian attempt to project regional power through sectarian proxies. In response to the Saudi request, the Pakistani parliament rejected the possibility of intervention by the Pakistani military and urged neutrality in the conflict, despite rhetorical support for the territorial integrity of Saudi Arabia. Although Pakistan has backed the United Nations Security Council resolution imposing an arms embargo on the Houthis, Pakistan's response may strain relations with Saudi Arabia and other Gulf States, and the spillover effects of the conflict threaten to aggravate Pakistan's pre-existing and growing sectarian tensions.

Civil-Military Relations in Pakistan

The recent tensions regarding alleged support by some in the military for the anti-government protests led by Imran Khan are but a symptom of a deeper and long-standing dysfunction within the civil-military relationship in Pakistan. A legacy of mistrust has hobbled foreign policy decision-making and effective management of internal security, a result from which neither side benefits.

The leadership of elected civilians in defining and executing Pakistani national security strategy is the central instrument for the formulation and implementation of a Pakistani foreign policy that can take advantage of the many regional opportunities available to Pakistan. This principle becomes even more important after the Peshawar attack as civilian dependence on the military to fight terrorism grows. The infrastructure of public policy-altering instruments built up by the formal national security institutions of Pakistan, the military and the intelligence services, is wide and pervasive and requires an intergenerational effort to be fully formalized and brought within the umbrella of accountability that should cover all publicly funded organizations in a democracy.

Both short- and long-term steps are needed for the Pakistani government to institutionalize a process whereby civilian and military leadership can meet to discuss pressing security issues as well as, over time, build confidence in the relationship and in civilian competence. This is especially true within Parliament whose role in foreign policy decision-making should eventually grow into one of proper oversight.

The Cabinet Committee on National Security and the National Security Division represent strong steps in the right direction. However, without assiduous stewardship by the top elected leaders in the country, further progress will remain elusive. Additionally, Pakistan needs to invest in long-term strategic planning capabilities to ensure its foreign policy priorities reflect the changes that have occurred and will continue to occur in the region and that the institutions that underpin foreign policy decision-making are properly resourced, staffed, and overseen by civilian leadership. This process must work in tandem with improving civilian-military coordination capacities. A commitment to sound strategic planning means questioning not only outdated assumptions, but also the bureaucratic processes that generated those assumptions.

Pakistan as a Responsible Nuclear Power

Pakistan's strategic perceptions both in the national security and economic realm focus on nuclear technology as instrumental to the future of the country. Such perceptions have fueled tensions in the region, arguably adding to a security dilemma marked by the asymmetries between India's conventional superiority and Pakistan's pursuit of asymmetric proxy warfare combined with a nuclear deterrent.

Pakistan's nuclear weapons program originally sought to counter India's conventional superiority and its pursuit of nuclear weapons in the 1970s. It was formally confirmed after the nuclear tests conducted in 1998 in response to India's testing of second-generation weapons. Until recently, Pakistan could defend its nuclear weapons program as being defensive in nature and rooted in the principle of deterrence.

Pakistan's intensive development of tactical nuclear weapons, however, has been interpreted as a fundamental shift in the nuclear equilibrium in South Asia. Analysts widely view this shift as being informed by the ever-growing difference in conventional power between Pakistan and India and the increased vulnerability Pakistan feels in any conflict that involves conventional warfare. This imbalance, combined with the fallout over the Abdul Qadeer Khan network, which trafficked Pakistan's nuclear secrets to North Korea, Iran, and Libya, fuel the international community's concerns over Pakistan as a responsible nuclear power. Tactical nuclear weapons expand the potential scope of nuclear weapons use to the battlefield and challenge the traditional view of nuclear weapons as strategic weapons of mass destruction. Tactical nuclear weapons represent a paradigm shift, not only in the strategic arena, but also in the operational space. Pakistan's shift toward tactical nuclear weapons, combined with its historical reliance on transnational militants to conduct asymmetric warfare and the fears of many observers about proliferation, therefore represents a source of international concern about early use of nuclear weapons or initiation of nuclear warfare by accident or miscalculation.

With respect to energy, nuclear power may represent a viable alternative to both traditionally high-cost hydrocarbons and low-cost but, in certain cases like the Kalabagh project, highly politicized hydroelectric power. In addition to existing nuclear power generation facilities in Karachi and Khushab, Pakistan has embarked on plans for as many as six new nuclear power reactors to be built within the next decade, with work on the first two having commenced in late 2013. Since the 1974 Indian nuclear weapons tests, which caused a cessation of nuclear power agreements between Pakistan and the United Kingdom and Pakistan and France respectively, the country's only consistent nuclear energy partner has been China. The latest reactors are being built with Chinese support.

The deterrence and the power generation arguments both represent deeply held, core-strategic pillars for Pakistan. The scope for international cooperation and engagement on nuclear nonproliferation, nuclear safety, and nuclear security takes place within the context of all the other major debates that engage issues of national security and economic growth. In short, on nuclear-related issues, the international community should seek out ways that build Pakistani confidence while Pakistan must commit itself to transparency in its nuclear programs and posture.

A clear opportunity to engage Pakistan exists based on the roadmap provided by India's experience with the Nuclear Suppliers Group waiver. As part of the U.S.-India civilian nuclear agreement in 2005, India placed its civilian nuclear facilities under International Atomic Energy Agency supervision while the agreement allowed it to separate its military program. Despite not being a party to the Nonproliferation Treaty or the Comprehensive Test Ban Treaty, the Nuclear Suppliers Group, which governs the export of nuclear technology, granted it a waiver for trade in technology. While the granting of the waiver caused a great deal of anger in Pakistan, some observers suggest it may be offered as a long-term inducement for further cooperation and openness by the Pakistanis on nuclear matters.

It would be an arduous process given credible complaints about Pakistan's proliferation history and concerns about its internal security. Taking as a starting point that Pakistan desires equity in treatment with India, the international community should show its willingness to consider a road map for a similar deal for Pakistan in return for serious nonproliferation and other concessions from Pakistan. Such a deal would be contingent on transparency, including Pakistan being much more forthcoming on the past activities of AQ Khan's network, to deal with the serious concerns in the international community over proliferation activities. Pakistan will need to take initial steps to build credibility and stability in Pakistan's relationships on this issue.

As part of a renewed bilateral dialogue, Pakistan and India could formalize their unilateral moratoria on testing. A future bilateral understanding could also serve to ensure the full de-mating (separation) of warheads and delivery vehicles, stationing weapons further from frontiers, improving civil control in Pakistan over weapons release, strengthening of existing permissive action links (PALs), and where possible developing new technologies to prevent accidental, insurgent, or criminal capacity to acquire and use nuclear weapons.

One goal may be for Pakistan to drop opposition to the Conference on Disarmament's program of work limiting the production of fissile material for nuclear weapons program. Both India and Pakistan maintain a minimum credible deterrence to each other's use of nuclear weapons. Further steps regarding confidence-building measures could then follow, including improved communications efforts and inspections (either joint or third-party-led).

Another goal would be to encourage a general de-escalation of nuclear tensions throughout the region. Like the United States, China has an interest in preventing an escalation of nuclear tensions in the region. A trilateral dialogue of India, China, and Pakistan could, in the future, serve to reinforce progress of whatever bilateral progress has taken place between India and Pakistan.

CHAPTER THREE

Violent Extremism

Since the U.S.-led intervention in Afghanistan in 2001, Pakistan's patronage of violent non-state actors has come to define not only its relationships with other countries, but also its fears of internal instability. Violent extremists have declared war on the Pakistani state and since 2007, when many smaller groups coalesced under the TTP umbrella, they have brutalized the Pakistani state and people. The TTP has positioned itself as an ally and host of international terrorists in Pakistan, including al Qaeda and, according to recent press reports, ISIS. The TTP is singularly unqualified and disinclined to play a role in Pakistani democratic politics and is only likely to survive as long as the current conflict in the frontier area.

Pakistan requires an urgent and sustained effort to push back against this offensive, an effort that not only addresses tactical considerations, but guides the totality of counterterrorism reforms. The *sine qua non* of this effort must be respect for Pakistan's constitutional and historical foundations as a modern, pluralistic state with a majority Muslim population. The North Waziristan operation was a first step in regaining momentum; the steps that come after it will define how permanent the gains are and how the costs, especially to the population, can be managed. Military offensives alone can, at best, disrupt terror networks, but are not a permanent solution.

The narratives that have developed in response to the evolving complexity of violent intolerance of diversity have been in some respects a cause of even greater alarm than the extremism itself. For years, terrorism analysts and counterterrorism experts advocated the use of groups more attuned with the syncretic strain of Islam more widely followed in South Asia and Pakistan against the rigid orthodoxy of alternative religious traditions such as Salafism. Yet these syncretic strains themselves cultivate a number of unapologetically violent and essentially anarchic impulses. Much to the chagrin of international experts who have long argued for employing the allegedly "soft" Barelvis against the "hard" Deobandis, the most passionate advocates of vigilante killings for alleged blasphemy turn out to be Barelvis. This is part of a broader widespread continuum of violent extremism across sects and groupings within mainstream Pakistani Islam.

This deeply upsetting and dangerous problem goes beyond the sects or groups themselves; it is the ease with which Pakistanis are now subject to lethal violence for holding any range of possibly "offensive" views. The core of the violent extremism problem in Pakistan is the unchecked and undeterred employment of violence with little or no reaction against voices of dissent and pluralism, especially attacks on secularists. There are many that argue forcefully that the problem is rooted in expecting religion, and, particularly Islam, to be an organizing framework for state and society. Yet Pakistan is hardly unique in this regard with many countries adopting Islam to varying degrees as an organizing framework for state and society.

If there is anything unique about Pakistan's relationship with Islam, it is that the state has systematically employed extremism as a tool of public policy both in the domestic and the foreign realm. This systematic use of extremism to mollify one constituency, motivate another, and scare yet another has endured across governments and leaders and, one could reasonably argue, across both military dictatorships and civilian democracies. There is little doubt however about the original source and abiding sustenance of this appetite for extremism as an instrument of public policy: it is rooted in the thinking of at least three generations of military and intelligence strategists. The damage this approach has done to Pakistan is now widely acknowledge in both civilian and military circles.

Three factors have inspired and fueled the sustenance of extremism as a public policy instrument. One, the military dictatorship of Zia ul-Haq explicitly and implicitly used extremism as a validating argument against democracy, setting a dangerous precedent for his successors. His policies were designed to transcend Pashtun nationalism by promoting a more transcendent identity to tamp down particularist or separatist tendencies. Two, geopolitical and budgetary advantages have accrued from investing in violent extremists to undertake acts beyond Pakistan's borders. And three, the investments in violent extremists have yielded at least two major tactical victories that have helped reinforce the appetite for them: first in Afghanistan when the Mujahideen successfully took on the Soviet armed forces, culminating in Moscow's retreat in 1988-89, and second, again in Afghanistan when the Taliban took power in 1996. There is a fear that the aftermath of the eventual drawdown of U.S. and foreign forces from Afghanistan will be the third instance in which irregular, non-state, violent extremists are able to win wars or at the very least preserve policy options for Pakistan.

There is, however, a growing and powerful counter-narrative to those that continue to see the employment of violent extremists as a useful instrument of public policy. Within the military and beyond, the mounting death toll from terrorist violence offers sobering evidence of the high costs of violent extremism. The economic fallout of Pakistan's suffering from terrorism is substantial, with the Economic Survey of Pakistan estimating the total direct and indirect costs at $102.5 billion.[1] The tearing of the social fabric is a palpable and widely acknowledged outcome of years of investing in extremists. Anti-Shi'a violence and sectarianism has been a particularly sore point for a country in which more than a fifth and according to some estimates as many as a third of all citizens are Shi'a.

The costs of violent extremism reach far beyond the domestic sphere. Pakistan's alleged patronage of violent extremists in the northwest such as the Haqqani Network complicates the country's relationship with Afghanistan, the United States, and the international community. Pakistan's alleged patronage of violent extremists in the Punjab heartland such as LeT complicates the country's relationship with India and other nations.[2] The impunity of anti-Shi'a groups such as the Lashkar-e-Jhangvi (LeJ) complicates relations between Pakistan and Shi'a-majority Iran as well.

In all, Pakistan is besieged by its violent extremism problem within its borders and gripped in a vise of complicated and tortuous relationships beyond its borders because of its violent extremism problem. It is difficult to conceive of any example of a more costly national strategic failure than Pakistan's failed romance with violent extremists as instruments of public policy. The Peshawar attack was only the most recent outcome of this policy seen especially in the promises by the government to no longer distinguish between good extremist groups and bad extremist groups. As Prime Minister Sharif stated in the wake of the attack, "We announce that there will be no differentiation between 'good' and 'bad' Taliban and have resolved to continue the war against terrorism till the last terrorist is eliminated."[3] If a policy shift on extremists is to be sustainable, it must extend to all non-state actors that threaten violence both within and beyond Pakistan. The lessons of the last decade must not be lost.

The rise of the TTP as a powerful, virulent, and violent anti-state terrorist coalition has not yet helped to engender clarity about the continued threat and risk from other violent extremist groups. Indeed, as Pakistan engages in a military offensive against the TTP, many are worried about the threat of retaliatory violence. The real worry, however, is much more fundamental. Ultimately, the key question in assessing the future of violent extremism in Pakistan will not be about the technicalities of the terms of a negotiation with terrorists, but rather the larger question of how groups negotiate power with the Pakistani state. Pakistan requires an urgent and uncompromising reassertion of state power in which the constitution and its associated norms—such as democracy, rule of law, and justice—are deemed supreme and above the narrow interests of any individual or group. The exercise of such power must be seen to have legitimacy, and for this to happen, the state must be able to deliver on its promises.

Extremism: A Regional Breakdown

Nationwide, FATA had the highest number of fatalities linked to violent extremism in 2014, according to the South Asia Terrorism Portal (SATP), with 2,863 fatalities; Sindh followed, with 1180, over 700 of them civilians; Balochistan had 653; Khyber Pakhtunkhwa had 617; and Punjab had only 180.[4] The figures were slightly lower than the previous year ascribed by SATP to previous military reluctance to engage the Taliban in North Waziristan.

Along with the ongoing problems in North Waziristan has been the increase in the number of terrorist groups such as LeJ, LeT, and Jaish-e Mohamed that operate nationwide. Activities of these groups range from attacks on Christians and Shi'a, in the case of Laskhar-e Jangvi, to terrorist attacks on the Indian parliament in 2001 and the Mumbai attacks of 2008, which included attacks on Jewish targets, conducted by LeT. Both of the Indian attacks resulted in severe strains on the fragile bilateral relationship and retaliatory military action by India was narrowly averted. Lingering frustration about the slow pace of the Pakistani legal system as well as state acquiescence in the activities of the Jamaat-ud-Dawa, the umbrella organization under which LeT operates, continues to rankle India. Alleged linkages of terrorists to the ISI remain a troubling aspect of the situation as does the virtual impunity of domestic terrorists. Linkages with the Taliban, whether financial or political, help these groups to function. At a minimum, the national focus on TTP and FATA relieves pressure to take action in relatively calm Punjab.

Karachi, Pakistan's economic and financial dynamo, remains the center of violent sectarian attack as well as of every other kind of civil and political unrest. The Pakistan Institute for Peace Studies has reported that there was a 53 percent increase in sectarian attacks in Pakistan in 2012, of which 85 percent took place in Karachi, Quetta, Kurram Agency, and Gilgit.[5] The institute gave a figure of 212 killed mainly in Karachi, but this may be a conservative estimate. One focused point of the attacks is the killing of Shi'a doctors. When police officials manage to crackdown on terrorists in Karachi they simply take refuge in Khyber Pakhtunkhwa and FATA as Karachi's top anti-terrorist police official, Chaudhry Aslam, pointed out shortly before his car bomb assassination on January 9, 2014. The TTP Mohmand Agency branch claimed responsibility for the killing. The terrorist killings take place amid a wider milieu of anarchy. The Human Rights Commission of Pakistan reported over 1,700 people killed in the city in the first half of 2013 alone.[6] In spite of controversial upgrades in security legislation under the Nawaz Sharif government, Karachi remains a nexus for criminal and terrorist activity with several sections of the city no-go zones and government largely invisible in many others.

The complex and interconnected layers of ethnic affiliations, political parties, criminal gangs, drug traders and fundamentalist terrorists make Pakistan's largest city and commercial center an entity that is both ungovernable but still critical to the national economy. Extra-legal actions and killings by security forces contribute to the climate of anarchy. Karachi is also the largest Pashtun city and third-largest Muslim city in the world. Karachi's more affluent residents spend their lives with gates, guards, and the constant fear of robbery, kidnapping, and murder. Narcotics trafficking, which provides income, access, and linkages is another element in the equation.

A solution to the problem of Taliban terrorism in northwestern Pakistan cannot be found unless there is a parallel process to contain terrorism in Karachi. Each space operates as a safe haven for the other and a conduit for materiel and finance. The military action against terrorism in FATA, especially in North Waziristan, may help mitigate the problem, but by itself will not solve the complex economic, ethnic, and political issues involved.

An overall counterterrorism strategy for Pakistan would ideally be aided by movement toward resolution of the Kashmir problem. The international community tends to minimize concentration on the issue in its discussions with Pakistan, where it is of essential importance. Pakistani-Indian relations cannot be firmly placed on an equitable and positive basis as long as the Kashmir issue remains unresolved. Some of the Punjabi-based terrorist groups are vehicles for the dangerous practice of maintaining pressure against India; revelations of Pakistani government involvement repeatedly surface. An improvement in relations with India brought about by mitigation of the Kashmir issue would remove the most substantial motivation for the terrorists' various sponsors in governmental structures to overlook or minimize their other activities. Another aspect of terrorism nationwide is the ambiguous connection with organized crime and the narcotics trade. These linkages make a counterterrorism strategy entrenched in the civilian sphere a high priority.

Provincial Connections

Resolution of the problems in FATA would begin to clear away some of the multifaceted connections that feed criminal and terrorist activities, but would only be the beginning. Economic and social issues will need to be addressed in the long run. As an example, the Sipah-i Sahaba group, from which the more extreme anti-Shi'a LeJ emerged, began as a movement in central Punjab by Sunni tenant farmers against their wealthy Shi'a landlords who in turn contain among their numbers prominent figures in Punjabi and national politics. The ramifications of terrorist acts in furtherance of their extremist Sunni goals cut across class, political, ethnic, and confessional lines, although they are primarily anti-Shi'a in nature.

The threat of a fundamentalist linkage across the northeast of the country into Kashmir and the rapid expansion of TTP control beyond their original base in FATA, which allowed them to threaten vital national infrastructure such as the Tarbela Dam, led the Pakistani military to move against terrorists in Swat in 2009.

Even before the offensive, many in Pakistan discounted the possibility of coming to an agreement or sustainable resolution with the Pakistani Taliban through talks arguing that no element of the TTP had a place in the politics of Pakistan. The fragmentation of the TTP under the threat of internal disagreements and Pakistani military action has not added clarity. During 2014, the TTP suffered three serious set-backs. The military operation in North Waziristan pushed its fighters out of their most convenient bases in Mir Ali and Miranshah. Counterterrorist actions in Pakistan's cities disrupted TTP sleeper cells and criminal fundraising. Finally, internal feuds and a leadership dispute led to many of the movement's most effective commanders forming the break-away group Jamaat ul Ahrar. While the TTP and its breakaways still command the loyalty of large numbers of militants, it can no longer claim to be a cohesive organization. However, elements of the TTP have partially compensated for their changing circumstances in Pakistan by securing a safe haven and freedom of movement in eastern and southeastern Afghanistan.

Role of Drones

Many influential Pakistanis see the United States as an aggressive player concerned mainly with its own issues in Afghanistan and one that targets indiscriminately with drones and consistently violates Pakistani territorial integrity whether by the killing of al Qaeda leader Osama Bin Laden or the undeclared deployment of Central Intelligence Agency (CIA) contractor Raymond Davis in Lahore. The latter led to an incredibly damaging fissure in the Pakistani-American relationship as well as myriad domestic implications within Pakistan, including the resignation of Foreign Minister Shah Mahmood Qureshi, now a leading PTI official. Washington's tactics have often met with Pakistani resistance, resulting in dissatisfaction and resentment on both sides. Popular disapproval of the United States—among the highest in the world—is directed at

American government policies and actions more than economic factors and personal relations. The drone program, controversial yet privately valued by Pakistani military officials, has across the board been criticized for mainly targeting terrorists who are active in Afghanistan although more recent attacks have targeted TTP leaders, especially in the wake of the Peshawar attack.[7]

U.S. cooperation in counterterrorism has become a charged issue in Pakistan's political discussions. After the Raymond Davis incident, the government of Pakistan radically restricted CIA operatives in the country. The tangled relations within the government of Pakistan and lack of clarity in the chain of command underlie many of Pakistan's problems in dealing with terrorism and with its counterterrorism cooperation with its international partners.

While the United States has been loath to compromise on its drone-based covert, CIA-led targeted killing program in Pakistan, facts on the ground have changed. With the drawdown of the bulk of U.S. and allied forces from Afghanistan, the use of drone strikes as an extended form of force protection has diminished, narrowing the scope of potential targets.

With respect to the Pakistani security establishment, it has long cooperated with the program, but the political calculus behind previous public opposition seems to be shifting with the offensive against the TTP. For one, the pace of drone strikes declined appreciably. From December 25, 2013, until June 11, 2014, there were no drone strikes within Pakistan proper,[8] evidently as the result of an agreement to curtail targeted killings while the Pakistani government pursued the prospect of peace negotiations with the TTP.[9] While the United States may have been privately skeptical of the Pakistani strategy, it was content to let events play out for the time being absent an opportunity to kill a high-value target such as members of the top al Qaeda leadership. That dynamic changed after the TTP attack on Karachi airport, which was followed by strikes that had the explicit blessing of the military and ISI.[10]

With the resumption of strikes, it would be prudent to see where the policy may be improved to reduce the attendant negative reaction to use of drones. If press reports are accurate that, in the course of supporting Pakistan's offensive, the Pakistani military is giving "express approval" for strikes against targets that are a threat to the Pakistani state, this may provide an opportunity to agree on best practices going forward. The recent convergence of interests around the program suggests that, while operations are unlikely to remain 100 percent joint, they might be for the majority of operations. Even if there were notable exceptions, an explicit joint approach would limit friction. The cost of continuing to hide behind official ambiguity is high enough to justify even initial steps to clarify the aims and operations of the program. While the exact specifics would be worked out in behind-the-scenes discussions between American and Pakistani diplomatic, military, and intelligence officials, it should include public acknowledgement of the justification for and nature of the program.

CHAPTER FOUR

A Cooperative South Asian Economic Region

Pakistan's geographical location places in it in a position to be an energy, trade, and economic development corridor for the entire region. There is already a large informal economy that operates across borders that needs to be formalized. The connections of population and location that cause tensions and have caused wars in the past could in a different equation serve as the means of unification and communication. Pakistanis share the languages they speak with each of their neighbors except China, and the widespread knowledge of Persian, Hindi-Urdu, Arabic, and English in Pakistan gives Pakistanis the opportunity to connect even wider internationally. The March 2014 decision of the PTI to change the language of instruction in Khyber Pakhtunkhwa to English in a transitional program reflects the political will to help the younger generations become more globally integrated.

The potential for trade relations between Pakistan and India is large. At present, only 0.5 percent of India's trade is with Pakistan and only 5.4 percent of Pakistan's trade is with India. The initial plans for Most Favored Nation status call only for trade through the existing Wagah border crossing in Punjab, with a further border post to be opened in Sindh next year. More border crossings, vastly improved transport and communication links, and wholesale modernization of the customs and border processing are necessary. The international community could play an important role in assisting Pakistan to modernize its antiquated bureaucracy. Corruption continues to be a main impediment to trade and travel. The Pakistani government has initiated programs to improve systems, but rapid modernization will send an important signal to Pakistan's neighbors that visible change is underway as well as providing for increased governmental revenues. There are numerous examples of countries that have made these changes that could be called upon to help.

Increased tensions between India and Pakistan since the middle of 2014 reinforce the urgency for normalizing relations. Of course, Pakistan cannot achieve all of this alone. However, there are clear policy measures that could help. Pakistan has still not given India permission to trans-ship merchandise to Afghanistan and on to Central Asia. Pakistan stands to benefit from such trade both financially and politically. Highways that link South Asia with Central Asia through Pakistan will become more and more necessary as Central Asia grows and changes and as the growing economies of South Asia seek new markets. Pakistan's important textile sector, for example, could be competitive in Central Asian markets, and its agricultural sector has an age-old connection with the cities there. Shared cultural, historic, and religious ties all make Pakistan and Pakistanis familiar in Central Asia.

Beyond the region, Pakistan has the potential to serve a much larger role in international trade. The extension of the European Union's Generalised Scheme of Preferences Plus (GSP+) can only be the first step in a process to tightly integrate Pakistan into the global trading regime and fully realize its potential as a hub not just for South Asia, but as a key trading partner for much of the rest of the world. Pakistan's partners such as the United States must reciprocate by ensuring access for Pakistani goods in their own markets. While a free trade agreement faces extremely high political hurdles in the United States, a near-term focus on a trade facilitation agreement represents a viable next step. Such an arrangement would allow for more robust technical and regulatory assistance and could eventually expand to include cross-border arrangements with Pakistan's neighbors. While not immediately feasible, both the European Union and the United States should identify a future roadmap for extending free trade policies to both India and Pakistan perhaps as a future extension to the Trans-Pacific Partnership (TPP), assuming that Pakistan and India have themselves normalized their trade relations. The United States could do much to encourage more contacts and understanding between U.S. and Pakistani business communities. This process should eventually include preferred access for Pakistan's textiles into U.S. markets.

A crucial adjunct to the development of a robust Pakistani economy is untangling the legacy of international financial assistance that has

enabled the state to survive a history of sub-par performance, as cata-
logued above. Non-collection of taxes and its attendant fiscal dysfunction means that foreign assistance underwrites an impressively wide
breadth of activities within Pakistan that should be the legitimate pur-
view of the Pakistani federal and provincial governments. Changing aid
priorities should be a priority step to allow Pakistan to reach its full economic potential.

To that end, Pakistan's bilateral partners and multilateral development and financial institutions should work with the Pakistani government to coordinate a narrower range of development programs. In
particular, there are three areas in which the problems to be addressed
are indeed beyond the reasonable bounds of the capacity of a developing country, at least in the short term: disaster management (including
water management), education, and health. International development
assistance organizations should coordinate with relevant Pakistani ministries to avoid duplication of efforts where particular agencies have
comparative advantages in certain regions or on specific issues and to
increase monitoring of discrete aid programs. International assistance
should encourage improvements in rule of law and accountability. Organizers of international assistance programs should develop a multi-year
roadmap that reflects the immediate needs of Pakistan and takes as its
goal the eventual end of large aid programs, consistent with the revenue
from future economic growth in Pakistan being returned to the Pakistani
government in the form of taxation.

Natural Resource Management

India and Pakistan share the waters of the Indus basin with Pakistan
receiving some 80 percent of the total. Although there have been some
problems over dam building and general utilization of resources to face
the problem of flooding and reduced flows, the overall performance of
the Indus water regime (regulated by the 1960 Indus Waters Treaty, or
IWT) has been successful. While tensions between India and Pakistan
have ebbed and flowed over the years, the consultations have continued,
making the IWT a remarkably durable agreement. The Indus waters
regime has been resilient and successful. Climate change, however,
promises to create serious problems in the future, of which the cata-
strophic floods in Pakistan in the past few years are only the beginning.

Experts predict a gradual decline in water availability coming from Tibet in the coming decades with water flows by 2060 predicted to be consistently less than in 2000 in the face of a vastly increased population. Pakistan and India need to work with China now to find ways to manage and cultivate water resources for the future. Pakistan's Water and Power Development Authority (WAPDA) developed a plan, Water Vision 2025, to construct five major dams and produce 16,000 megawatts of electricity. Careful attention needs to be given to financing, implementation, and evaluation of the future of the project. Pakistan must take into account reduced water yields due to climate change, and growing needs from an increasing population.

Along with Most Favored Nation status, Pakistan and India may sign an agreement for Pakistan to import 1,200 MW of electricity from India annually with initial studies to be financed by the World Bank. Such an agreement would not only help to relieve Pakistan's chronic energy shortages that cripple its industrial economy and reduce its growth rate by perhaps half, but also help to maintain peaceful relations between the two nations as any such line would be vulnerable to political and security vicissitudes to the disadvantage of both parties. These developments would require an improvement in bilateral relations. While the current political context is not encouraging, it is crucial not to lose sight of such opportunities.

Two other regional projects designed to help Pakistan's energy shortfall are the Turkmenistan–Afghanistan–Pakistan–India (TAPI) pipeline project and the 1000 Electricity Transmission and Trade Project for Central Asia and South Asia (CASA-1000 project). The first is a gas pipeline designed to bring energy from Turkmenistan through Afghanistan to Pakistan and India. If completed on schedule in 2018, it would alleviate up to 25 percent of Pakistan's energy gap. The project, which now may cost more than $10 billion, would pass through southern Afghanistan and the Pakistani province of Balochistan, areas where local insurgencies and al Qaeda and the Taliban have strong presences. Baloch nationalists continue to attack gas pipelines and the electric grid in Pakistan. The company most interested in running the pipelines, Exxon-Mobil, is U.S.-owned, adding to the security risk. The United States has been strongly in favor of the pipeline.

The other energy resource in planning is the Central Asia South Asia Project CASA-1000, also supported by the United States. The project entails energy cooperation among Kyrgyzstan, Tajikistan, Afghanistan, and Pakistan, and would supply Pakistan with 1,000 megawatts of electricity from summer hydropower surplus in Central Asia. Financing of $1 billion has been provided by the World Bank and the Islamic Development Fund for the project, scheduled to begin operations in 2016.

Afghanistan and Pakistan are also planning to share the electricity from a 1,600 megawatt dam to be built on the Kunar River, a major tributary of the Kabul River which supplies significant water to Pakistan, particularly in summer. Capitalizing on this requires the building of the requisite legal framework to cover the sharing of the Kabul River, which does not yet exist.

Sustainable Development

While discussions of economic development are essential to any process of improving policy both internationally and within Pakistan it is essential that such steps are crafted in a sustainable manner. Not only would the introduction of a climate focus aid in policymaking for Pakistanis, but it also would be a critical priority for expanding regional cooperation. It is an argument that underscores the case for joint cooperation on energy security as the prospect that anthropogenic (man-made) climate change will negatively impact economic and humanitarian development throughout the region. In addition to the tragic loss of life, the devastating floods that struck Pakistan in 2010 demonstrated the impact of environmental risk on the country's economy and infrastructure. While it is difficult to tie the severity of any single disaster to climate change, the Intergovernmental Panel on Climate Change (IPCC) has consistently warned that flooding of this type will likely become worse over time.[1] The region has also seen how annual flooding has impacted Bangladesh. In a scenario of rapid climate change the region could see massive refugee flows as areas become uninhabitable.[2]

It is hoped that this threat, which crosses borders, can motivate interested parties to build a durable record of cooperation. The countries of the region have an interest in adopting national climate change policies, not only to respond to crises, but also to build future resiliency. In Pakistan, a national climate change policy needs to be developed alongside provincial responsibilities derived from the Eighteenth Amendment. All have interests in building green economies for the benefit in slowing global climate change and also for making the local environment cleaner for their respective citizens. In the context of global climate change mitigation what happens in South and East Asia will have a determining effect on how severe future warming patterns will be. If a business-as-usual approach continues, economic growth on the subcontinent will lead to a rapid rise in emissions and a likely breaking through of the world's remaining carbon budget.[3]

In addition to sharing a border and critically important river system, India and Pakistan share the perspective of developing nations that are trying to balance the necessity of aggressive economic growth with protecting fragile ecological resources. While India's growth statistics over the past decade have been more robust than Pakistan's, it will likely be following a similar path, raising questions about how to achieve sustainable growth. Actions taken by both nations in international fora such as the 2015 meeting of the United Nations Framework Convention on Climate Change (UNFCC) in Paris will be critical. As poor nations, the expectations that they will have to drastically cut emissions are much different than for the United States or the European Union. Their focus will likely be on how to coordinate with wealthier nations on aid and assistance to achieve green growth, through low- or zero-carbon sources of electricity generation, smart grid investments, energy efficiency gains, and many other goals identified by climate change experts as the kinds of investments that are necessary for developing world nations to make the leap to growing economies that are sustainable and avoid the previous, higher emission levels of carbon dioxide.

Recent polling suggests that such cooperation could be well received by India and Pakistan.[4] In a 2013 poll by the Australian-based Lowy Institute, 83 percent of Indians identified climate change as a big threat over the next ten years. Concerns about energy, water, and food shortages (in addition to climate change generally) were placed ahead of any traditional state-centered security threat. A 2013 research survey in Pakistan looked at how a sampling of 4,000 Pakistanis thought about climate and sustainability issues.[5] While knowledge of climate change *per se* was weak, many people did report concerns about food and water security. While reduced electricity availability was widely recognized, reduced water availability was also a widely cited problem with majorities noticing reduced availability in Balochistan (80 percent); Khyber Pakhtunkwa (53 percent); and Sindh provinces (52 percent).[6] Unsurprisingly, vast majorities of those surveyed did not trust the established government at the national, provincial, or local level to deal with the issue. Only local neighborhood support garnered any confidence.[7] While this sample is only two polls, it suggests rising public concern for how climate change may affect the subcontinent.

The crisis over the loss of life from drought conditions in Tharparkar district is instructive. A desert region in Sindh province, Tharparkar has seen over one hundred recent deaths, mostly children, from starvation. Overall, 650 people died of starvation in the area as of the end of 2014. The government quickly announced an aid package of 1.5 billion PKR. Such a financial outlay can only be thought of as an emergency measure to be followed up by further changes in government and adoption of more robust development priorities. Otherwise, tragedies like that in Tharparkar are likely to recur.[8] Another area in which climate change may bring together nations in the region is how to make urban growth sustainable. The future of South Asia is likely urban, a trend that is reflected around the world as agricultural productivity rises, pushing labor into cities.

Analysts have often cited the varied deficiencies in Pakistan's energy sector as a drag on its growth ("the largest single drain on [its] economy" in the estimation of Pakistan's Ministry of Finance, responsible for reducing gross domestic product by two percent per year[9]) and a contributing factor to pessimism about its governance capacity. Constant load-shedding has been a fact of life for urban Pakistanis for several years now. As the temperature rises in urban areas in Pakistan, twelve-hour downtimes become a regular fact of life.[10] Not only do electricity outages stem from supply issues, but also from general management difficulties within the companies operating in Pakistan's power sector with losses in transmission and distribution. Non-payment of electricity fees draws away important revenue from Pakistan's treasury, and the importation of fossil fuels negatively impacts trade balances. Combined with generous subsidies, the fiscal challenges are enormous. According to one analyst, in 2011-12, WAPDA, the largest power and water utility, and the Karachi Electrical Supply Corporation cost the Pakistani government as much as its armed forces.[11]

If the international community is serious in its efforts to get Pakistan's economy back to work, it should prioritize its efforts to build cooperation on energy issues, including consistent requirements for reform of pricing and revenue collection as a prerequisite for cooperation on facilitating the introduction of higher-value sources of power generation. Assessing areas where U.S. and international assistance can have the largest effect will ideally identify goals and benchmarks that are realistic and would benefit from input from Pakistanis. Targeting specific benchmarks—for example, cutting the time the grid is load-shedding—would allow for the government to quickly demonstrate capacity.

Joint energy cooperation was highlighted as a key area of focus for U.S. assistance to Pakistan when Prime Minister Sharif met with President Obama in October 2013.[12] As part of the efforts of the U.S.-Pakistan Energy Working Group, officials from both countries will consider a technical assistance program focused on the further exploitation of Pakistan's limited natural gas reserves. As it stands, less than 30 percent of power generation is derived from natural gas, which burns cleaner than coal or oil.[13]

Another potential option for relieving the energy crisis is finding space for increasing use of renewable energy. Currently, Pakistan's energy mix still privileges fossil fuels and hydroelectric. The Pakistani government needs to think through how to diversify its sources of electrical generation. In response to a question in the National Assembly, the federal minister for petroleum and natural resources, Shahid Khaqan Abbasi, admitted that at the current rate of consumption the country only had about sixteen years of natural gas reserves remaining.[14] While the government has responded by working with foreign companies and other governments to accelerate domestic exploration and exploitation, much of the work has been delayed by security concerns. Other projects, through partnerships with China and Qatar, are looking to expand Pakistan's hydropower capacity.[15]

Over the long-term, however, Pakistan will need to expand these efforts, taking into account not only building up hydropower, but also nuclear and renewables. This process will be expensive, and subject to difficult political decision-making at the federal and provincial level. Pakistan's use of non-hydroelectric renewables (solar[16] and wind) lags behind India's. The recent announcement that the government would eliminate tariffs on imported solar equipment, and allow grid integration of different solar power installations, including at-home rooftop panels, is an excellent first step.[17] A few pilot projects in solar, wind, and tidal have been undertaken, but further expansion requires reform of the utility sector and of pricing and tariff structures.

There is very little reason not to pursue closer energy cooperation within the wider context of building regional cooperation. The United States maintains a robust bilateral energy dialogue separately with India and Pakistan. As a strategy for encouraging and rewarding efforts to stabilize relations with each, the United States should add a trilateral component incorporating representatives to address issues common to all three nations. Such an initiative need not prejudice the important issues that exist on a bilateral basis. Rather, a trilateral energy dialogue would be in addition to existing discussion efforts. The agenda for the most recent U.S.-India dialogue, for example, included discussions of regional energy cooperation.[18] Such planning discussions are crucial, but need to be followed up by interactions in multilateral settings. The hope in doing so is that technical progress on shared energy goals can be sustained at a political level and that the United States can use its role to facilitate difficult discussion and potential negotiations over cross-border projects.

Potential breakthroughs in the South Asian context will benefit more than just the populations of the nations in question. It would be hoped that the best practices derived from such efforts could be applicable to other regions where legacies of conflict and political tension have prevented meaningful progress on cross-border cooperation on issues as sensitive to national interest as energy security. The Congo River Basin, where Pakistan and India have sent a combined 8,000 peacekeepers in support of the United Nations Organization Stabilization Mission in the Democratic Republic of the Congo (MONUSCO), is only one such example.[19] The international community would thus benefit immeasurably from the usage of energy security to bring together previously difficult-to-reconcile neighbors.

The tensions between the Islamic Republic of Iran and the international community (principally the United States and major powers within the European Union) over Iran's nuclear program have had a negative impact on Pakistan's energy trajectory. With progress toward a nuclear deal between Iran and the P5+1, there is potential for cooperation. As part of a normalization of relations between Iran and its international interlocutors, preliminary discussions should begin about how to remove as a priority the sanctions against the Iran-Pakistan pipeline.

CHAPTER FIVE

Internal Governance Reform

In addition to a complex regional political and economic dynamic, exacerbated by a profound internal militancy challenge, the Pakistani state itself faces myriad challenges in administering law and order in the entirety of its territory, aggressively expanding economic growth, providing its citizens with the human capital necessary to compete globally, and protecting the rights of minorities. Several initiatives under the broad heading of governance reform have been recommended by a variety of actors, both internal and external. While events in the region make for propitious timing for shifts regional and foreign policy, the time has also come for corresponding shifts in internal governance.

Inclusive Administrative Reform

Balochistan is one of Pakistan's most troubled areas. Rich in natural resources, especially gas, Balochistan is also the poorest of Pakistan's provinces in per capita income. The perception of a lack of equitable distribution of resources is one main resentment that the Baloch have toward Islamabad. Balochistan is also Pakistan's largest province, with 46 percent of the territory and its least inhabited with only 5 percent of the population. The Baloch Liberation Army, the latest incarnation of Baloch resistance to the state, carries out armed attacks in the province aimed at non-Baloch settlers, the Pakistani state, and the province's natural resources. It attacked the electric grid three times in January 2015, culminating in a January 25 attack that left 80 percent of the country without electricity, including all major cities and the capital. In April 2015, an attack on a laborers' camp near Turbat resulted in the deaths of a least twenty dam construction workers.

In addition, LeJ and Sepah-e Sahaba have an ongoing campaign of attacks against Shi'a in Balochistan and other areas, but especially in Quetta. Two attacks in early 2013 that killed nearly two hundred resulted in the dismissal of the elected provincial governor and his replacement with an Islamabad appointee. There have been hundreds of cases of disappearances of individuals and torture is commonplace. The Baloch contend that their province has been treated as a colony by Islamabad with more soldiers than teachers, and large numbers of military bases. Human rights observers have made complaints about the practices of both the Baloch insurgents and government forces. Pakistan has asserted that various foreign powers, in particular India, are behind Baloch terrorist attacks as part of a plan to break up Pakistan. The Baloch people, who are mainly Sunni and speak a language related to Farsi, extend beyond Pakistan's borders into southern Afghanistan and Iran. Iran and Pakistan have an interest in strongly asserting their governmental authority over their respective provinces of Balochistan, and Iran has spoken out strongly against Sunni terrorist attacks on its border officials.

Prime Minister Sharif has the opportunity to create a new relationship with Balochistan based on a civilian rather than military mindset. Development of the extraordinary potential of Balochistan's resources is not only critical for Pakistan and the region, it could also provide more than ample income for the people of Balochistan. One of Pakistan's main economic impediments is the lack of energy availability. A competently governed Balochistan can provide that. In addition, a Balochistan that is stable can also be the avenue for other ventures, such as the planned pipelines to bring energy from Iran and Turkmenistan and down-the-road transport and energy development connected with the Chinese-run port at Gwadar. Foreign investors will expect Pakistan to establish security and stability in Balochistan prior to directing capital to the province.

Ending the violence in Balochistan will take flexibility and negotiation at a time when Islamabad is preoccupied with the TTP in the northwest and when the Pakistani military has been reluctant to allow civilian authorities the necessary leeway to negotiate. However, a Balochistan that is not restive against the national government could then over time free up thousands of Pakistani army troops to be used elsewhere. The changes would require a strategic governance vision for Pakistan based on a holistic progression, rather than a sequential zero-sum game that rewards one or two groups at the cost of others.

Federally Administered Tribal Areas (FATA)

The reform process for FATA should be encouraged. With the incursion of the Taliban and replacement of the malik system in certain areas, the agent-malik system of government going back to the British Raj needs change, which Pakistan and the peoples of FATA have recognized. Economic, judicial, and social reforms are imperative to undercut Taliban influence in the region, which still has an overall literacy rate of only 21.4 percent and only 7.5 percent among females. Lack of work, poverty, and low social indicators compounded with an outmoded and corrupt administrative regime made the tribal peoples susceptible to both the message of the Taliban and the income they received from providing food and shelter to foreign "guests." Pakistan should be encouraged to regularize the status of the region where laws passed in Islamabad are only applicable at presidential discretion. The United States and other donors should stand ready to help and finance reforms in the region, but allow the tribal peoples and other Pakistanis to be the visible managers of change. While unlikely in the current context, any future negotiations with TTP groups must strike a careful balance between national sovereignty and local autonomy in a difficult context that threatens international security.

Financing Pakistan

Pakistan's economy is twenty-fifth in the world in terms of purchasing power, and forty-fourth in dollar terms. The large economy, and even larger potential, has been undermined by a population of 200 million that continues to grow rapidly. The costs of war and natural disasters have also severely impacted the development potential of the country. In terms of government revenue, Pakistan receives a much lower percentage of its income from taxes than might be expected (8.5 percent of GDP), placing it on the level of countries such as Ethiopia and Afghanistan, which have a much lower GDP. A UK government report in 2013 claimed that only 0.57 percent of people in the country actually paid taxes at all ﹑

the previous year.[1] Only recently have legislators been required to file income tax returns. The government had to revise its revenue forecast downward in March of 2014, cutting its public sector development program from 540 million rupees to 425 million in spite of economic growth in the first quarter of the year calculated at 5 percent and an announced decrease in inflation of one percentage point, down to 7.5 percent.

The income that the government does derive from taxation comes mainly from VAT and additional taxes advocated by the IMF and other international financial institutions (IFIs), which Pakistani organizations claim have favored the elite by reducing their taxes 15 percent while lower class taxpayers suffered an increase of 7.5 percent. Taxes on agricultural land are a provincial subject in Pakistan, but the federal government estimates that such revenues are as little as 1 percent of the potential. Any effort to improve Pakistan's economy must deal with the difficult topic of taxes, which is made more difficult by the presence of many of the largest potential taxpayers in the provincial and national assemblies. Administration of the tax regime is also a difficult topic when related to overall questions of governance, particularly on the provincial and district levels. Turkey might offer an example of a country that is in a successful program of modernizing and systematizing tax collection and that has its own history of dealing with IFIs.

Federal Finance Minister Ishaq Dar gave an optimistic three-year projection of Pakistan's potential for progress on March 3, 2014, consonant with the requirements of the $6.64 billion loan the IMF approved as a last resort to stave off financial collapse. Dar's targets are an increase in the GDP growth rate from 3 percent to 7 percent, in the tax ratio to the GDP from 8.5 percent to 13.0 percent, and a lowering of the deficit from 8.8 percent to 4.0 percent. It remains to be seen if the targets will be met. Notwithstanding the decrease in revenue that led to the lowering of tax targets, the government claimed an increase of tax collection of 25 percent in January 2014. It moved forward on the issuing of $2 billion in Euro bonds in April of 2014.[2] Foreign reserves reached $15 billion in January 2015, and foreign workers' remittances totaled $9 billion in 2014, according to the Pakistan Bureau of Resources. Pakistan received the first $550 million tranche from the new loan in March 2014, plus a payment of $350 million from the United States in Coalition Support Funds and a second tranche of $1.05 billion in December 2014 that had been delayed by the anti-government protests organized by Imran Khan.[3] Pakistan gained $1.12 billion from the sale of telecom licenses in 2014, as well as another $1.5 billion by June 2015, forecasted from the privatization of government enterprises, the latter was also advocated by the IMF. The U.S. government assistance request for Pakistan for fiscal year 2015 is $1.882 billion, including $1 billion in Coalition Support Funds.

The Asian Development Bank (ADB) has stressed in its new business plan with Pakistan the need for fiscal balance, sustained growth, and increased investment and policy reforms. It also underlines the priorities of improved transport, regional connectivity, improved irrigation and urban services. It will lend Pakistan a total $3.256 billion over the next three years in programs designed for investment and policy reform to make state enterprises more efficient. About 28 percent of the loans will be in multi-tranche facilities and projects have been proposed for Balochistan and Khyber Pakhtunkhwa.

Pakistan's external debt now stands at some $60 billion dollars and servicing costs keep rising. The IMF loan of $6.64 billion in September 2013 saved Pakistan then, but it is clear that the syndrome of ongoing increasing debt and service is not tenable for the long run. Some Pakistanis have called for debt forgiveness, pointing to numerous other countries that have received that benefit. Pakistan's war costs were assessed by the finance ministry at $67.9 billion in 2011, more than Pakistan's external debt. In addition, the war has discouraged investment in Pakistan leaving the investment to GDP ratio to decline from 22.5 percent in 2007 to 14 percent in 2013. In India, it was 35 percent and in Iran, in spite of international sanctions, 31 percent. If the international community wishes to truly turn Pakistan around, it could take action on this issue. For this to happen, Pakistan would need to make changes in governmental processes and accountability, clarify lines of command and the implementation of assistance moneys. Accountability and corruption remains a serious problem within Pakistan on many levels and is a major concern to the donor community.

Economic governance in Pakistan's federal system remains seriously troubled and troubling for the international community. Incandescent tales of corruption in Pakistan appear frequently in the Pakistani and international press, further fuelling much of the disillusionment with democracy among the country's youth. The legitimacy of any civilian government will hinge to a great extent on the willingness to acknowledge the scope of corruption and undertake serious and sustained anti-corruption efforts. Pakistan's democratically elected government has the opportunity to make radical changes and the pre-election government program contained a long list of governance reforms it planned to implement. Transparency International gives Pakistan a poor rating in its Corruption Perceptions Index.[4] In global competitiveness, it comes in at 129 out of 144 countries,[5] and at 146 out of 187 in human development.[6] And in press freedom, in spite of a vocally critical English language press it is ranked at only 158 out of 180.[7] A great deal of the vexing nature of the corruption problem in Pakistan is that so much of it is built into the day-to-day operation of the political system. From price rigging to favoritism, many of the practices are deeply ingrained into how elites leverage and expand their power.

The areas for improvement are fairly clear: tax administration, procurement, devolution of powers to local administration in education, health, roads and other services, civil service reform, and a long-term effort to stem corruption. The latter, perhaps, the most important, can only be done by a consensus of opinion on the part of the Pakistani establishment—the government, army, and the industrial/landowning elites. Years of failure to deal with the problem through a succession of dictatorships has resulted in a country that many consider a failing state. As a basic step to remedying these deficiencies, the Prime Minister's Office, working with the Council on Common Interests, should provide the necessary financial and staff resources to enable the achievement of the Planning Commission's Vision 2025 goals.

Control of corruption is imperative for development and governmental structures, such as the National Accountability Bureau and the Ombudsman's office, which need to be strengthened and the civil service reformed, but there are also immediate steps that can start to work against corruption. Among these are eliminating conflict of interest, transparency in government actions (especially procurement), oversight of government officials, and using available tools such as the Freedom of Information act to serve as watchdog over government actions.

Education

At the core of Pakistan's multiple dysfunctions is an education system so badly broken and neglected that it condemns more than 25 million children between the ages of 5 and 16 to being out of school. The Pakistani children that are in school receive a substandard education by every government and nongovernmental measure available.[8] The governance of public schools is shambolic, with endemic teacher absenteeism and large-scale corruption in school construction projects. The regulation of private schools, a sector that has grown explosively, is virtually nonexistent. This produces a wide array of curricula to be taught across class, geography, and the rural-urban divide. The education system of the country, which should be an instrument of healing and progress, is instead responsible for the shrinking space for pluralism and widening indignity of Pakistan's poor and dispossessed. The poorest and most vulnerable Pakistanis are the ones whose children are left furthest behind in a Pakistan that lacks sufficient interest in educating its children.

Experts agree that the entire system is in need of reform and some indicators of progress seem to be coalescing. Over the past five years, Punjab, Pakistan's most populous province, has undertaken significant expense and effort to solve the teacher absenteeism problem and widen the net of children in school.[9] In Khyber Pakhtunkhwa, which is most harshly affected by terrorism, the PTI-led government has initiated an array of reforms.[10] Yet these efforts sit at the periphery of political discourse and budgetary allocations continue to be shamefully low. Pakistan is ranked at 172 in the world in terms of the share of GDP that it spends on education, hovering at 2 percent.[11] Promises to raise this are now a decade old, but hardly any movement has occurred.

Given the desperate state of primary, middle, and secondary schooling, it is not surprising that only 5.1 percent of Pakistani students are in higher education—compared to 18 percent in India and 42 percent in Malaysia.[12] The outmoded school system produces incompetent graduates who are incapable of participating in the competitive business sector, and thus risk becoming dependent on state patronage; this trend is exacerbated by an economy that cannot produce private sector jobs fast enough to keep pace with population growth. Government jobs, salaries, and pensions are the fastest growing entities in Pakistan's economy and budget and they have been thus for decades. The impact of this is cyclical and tragic. The highest number of government jobs are in teaching, and so Pakistan continues to burden its treasury with the salaries and pensions of growing numbers of under-qualified, demotivated, and

unaccountable teachers. They produce the very low-quality learning outcomes that then make their students unemployable. It is a continuing
cycle that hobbles Pakistan's potential for growth.

Pakistan has the kind of youth bulge that supported the industrializa-
tion of neighboring countries; however, the populations in question were
at higher educational levels. Unfortunately, failure to finance education
at all levels has produced a population that is lacking in contemporary
skills and capabilities. Substandard schools and health standards mean
that the young population is not prepared to meet the challenges of a
twenty-first century economy. Literacy remains at unacceptable levels.
The government estimates it at 57 percent nationwide, 69 percent for
males and 45 percent for females, with figures for the latter demographic
sinking to only single digits in some rural areas.[13] Nationwide, almost half
of those aged 5 to 16 are not in school, school standards are substantially
below par, and the primary school dropout rate exceeds 30 percent. The
growing numbers of private schools, particularly in rural areas, do not fill
the gap in government schooling in either numbers or quality. The inter-
nationalization of efforts to include the madrasas in the national educational mainstream and the proliferation of international programs to
modernize and standardize the curricula of madrasas have been used as
excuses by successive governments to stall reform—citing the opposition
of the radical right wing within and beyond the political mainstream.

Pakistan has the ability to change this, and a massive infrastructure
of international support already exists. Yet, any change in education
demands substantial and sustained political leadership. Pakistan does not
have anything akin to a national discourse on education or on education
reform. Most of the policy debate in education is underwritten by Western donors. This is why, in part, efforts to regularize religious madrasas
and incorporate them into the mainstream have largely failed. No country
can afford to outsource the conversation about its future to the philan-
thropy of foreign governments and international assistance bureaucrats,
but that is exactly what Pakistan has done. Making the curricula more
relevant to Pakistan's needs, upgrading the quality of teaching, institut-
ing accountability for education managers and administrators, and fixing
broken school infrastructure are urgent needs. Where possible, Pakistan
should be able to work with non-Western nations and school systems to
identify practices in funding mechanism, revising the general curriculum,
with a particular focus on increasing tolerance. The clear goal, however,

should be a plan to replace completely foreign funding in the education sector. As a first step, Pakistan should fulfill its promise to spend at least 4 percent of its GDP on education in order to meet the demands of the National Plan for Action for Education presented by Prime Minister Sharif to the United Nations General Assembly side session on education in September 2013.[14] This will help address the enrollment of millions of out of school children, especially girls. If Pakistan does not develop an indigenous and politically feasible national discourse around these needs, it has little chance of succeeding in overcoming any of the broader economic, political, and security challenges it faces.

Capitalizing on Pakistan's Demographic Trends

Pakistan's demographic situation is a key challenge, even with improvement in energy and infrastructure. It is the sixth most populous country in the world and is well on the way to becoming the fourth with the highest birth and fertility indices in South Asia. Between 1990 and 2008, Pakistan's population increased by 54 percent as compared to a 34 percent increase for India in the same period. Its population of 200 million is likely to exceed 300 million by 2050. This demographic trend reflects the weak position of women. Use of contraceptives is at a low level, reaching only 29.5 percent of the population in Sindh and 19.5 percent in Balochistan. The highest usage level is in the Islamabad Federal District and that is only 59.4 percent. Unless women in general are more empowered economically and socially, growing urbanization in Pakistan does not necessarily result in lowered birth rates and this means a corresponding increase in discontented urban young people seeking employment.

Pakistan is home to one of the world's youngest populations. Two of every three Pakistanis are under the age of 30.[15] This "youth bulge" has not gone unnoticed. Pakistani advertisers and Pakistani politicians have caught on and the dominant drivers in both the high-consumption urban economy and the overall political discourse reflect a robust consciousness that the biggest population segment in the country is young people. The core of advertising and marketing in Pakistan focuses on this youth population.[16] The 2013 general election was hailed as Pakistan's "youth" election. The demographic estimates suggest that all elections in Pakistan will continue to be "youth" elections now until about the middle of this century with the "youth bulge" expected to ease around 2045.[17]

The context within which violence-promoting madrasas have flourished is the complete abdication by the state of its responsibility to care for Pakistani children. One way to contextualize this beyond Pakistan's shocking education statistics is to consider the state of child nutrition in the country. Of children under the age of five, 45 percent are too short for their age, 30 percent are underweight, 11 percent are too thin for their height, and 25 percent are born with low birth weight (less than 2.5 kilograms).[18] This is a direct result of poor nutrition—of mothers, infants and children. A large percentage of madrasa students enroll in these schools because of the abject poverty of their families.

A range of instruments already in place, but poorly executed, could address extreme poverty and malnutrition. Pakistan has several social protection mechanisms, including the Benazir Income Support Program, the Baitul Mal Fund, and the Zakaat Fund, which award cash grants to the poorest and most vulnerable Pakistanis—yet they have failed to penetrate communities where violent extremists are routinely able to make inroads, recruit fighters, and enroll unwitting children into violence-promoting madrasas. It is important to note, however, as recent research into LeT recruiting has shown, that Pakistan's non-religious education institutions are also effective incubators for extremism.[19] In fact, some research suggests that Islamic militants are better educated on average than other Pakistanis.[20]

Pakistan has one of the lowest rates of Internet connectivity in Asia; 10.9 users for every 100 inhabitants compared to 15.1 per 100 for India and 84.8 per 100 for South Korea.[21] One popular and effective measure that the Punjab Chief Minister Shahbaz Sharif (the prime minister's brother and close confidante) initiated in 2011 was to provide free laptops and Internet connections to young high school and university students. With increased connectivity, Pakistani students could enroll in global free university programs and obtain education not otherwise available to them. Online education on the technical and professional level already extant on the web could be redesigned for specific Pakistani employment needs. Again, the Punjab government has been leading on this, with the launch in January 2014 of an e-learning portal that provides online material for school curricula.[22]

Access to the Internet has the potential to make a positive contribution to Pakistan, but it also carries the risk of providing an outlet for fundamentalist propaganda and hate speech.[23] The government of Pakistan needs to commit itself to programming that is non-sectarian and non-propagandistic in nature. Recent literature festivals in Lahore and Karachi drew tens of thousands of participants, many of them young people, but sponsors complained that any such efforts are immediately attacked by Islamic extremists as atheistic and sponsored by the decadent West. The failure on the part of public officials to speak out, no doubt because they have been intimidated by violence and murders, has to be addressed if Pakistan is to hold together. Postponing action or ignoring issues is no longer viable for Pakistan. Pakistanis of the upper and middle classes can no longer ignore what is going on outside their garden walls or as in the case of Bin Laden what is going on inside their neighbors' walls.

Pakistan's youth bulge is actually the majority of the nation. Meanwhile, the nation's political leadership is increasingly elderly, isolated, and myopic. The reason for the widespread popularity of Imran Khan's PTI is that he is perceived to be an independent voice that does not stand for the political establishment that has run Pakistan's politics for decades. The generation that grew up in the shadow of British India has disappeared, and their place in the Pakistani imagination has been taken to a large extent by ideologues influenced by fundamentalist Islam. Pakistani leaders need to renew and revise their thinking if they wish to see the Pakistan that they recognize continue. This means a commitment to education and equality to create a Pakistan of equal opportunity and optimism rather than a tapestry of decline and despair woven in nostalgia for a class system that strangles progress.

Improving the Role for Women

Individual women in Pakistan have had high profiles. Benazir Bhutto, first female Prime Minister of a Muslim country, will remain one of the more prominent figures of the twentieth century. Pakistan has had a successful female foreign minister, ambassadors, judges, human rights activists, artists, authors, professors, and public figures. Over 20 percent of Pakistani parliamentarians are women, largely serving in seats reserved for them, a figure that places the country behind only Nepal and Afghanistan in South Asia.[24] There are many prominent women of whom Pakistan is rightly proud. But there is a price. Benazir Bhutto was murdered,

Punjabi Minister Zilla Huma Usman was assassinated, the schoolgirl and Nobel Peace Prize laureate Malala Yousafzai has been vilified even after almost being killed, and there are countless other women who have been victims of violence and discrimination. While a limited number of women in urban areas, particularly in elite circles, speak freely and have professional and public careers, the same is not true for the vast majority, particularly in the countryside. If, by an optimistic standard, over 30 percent of Pakistani women work outside their homes, 60 percent of those working are in the agricultural sector, frequently with no compensation. Taliban actions against girls' schools are well known outside Pakistan, but lack of education, particularly higher education for girls is prevalent throughout Pakistan. Of Pakistan's 25 million out-of-school children more than 15 million are girls.

Pakistan has endorsed the goal of achieving gender equality by 2015 in the Millennium Development Goals. Like many of the other standards it will not be met and Pakistan has to do much more to equal even the efforts of its South Asian neighbors. To develop, Pakistan must educate and empower its women. Bureaucratic reluctance to reform coupled with corruption particularly affects uneducated women who do not know how to demand their rights. Some in Pakistan work to advance the rights of women, and considerable though patchy progress has been made in recent years, but lack of political will, bureaucratic inertia, and low budgeting of equality initiatives still signify women's development as a secondary priority. The growth of religious extremism also particularly affects individual human rights for women many of whom have seen their freedom of movement and more generally their possibilities to shape their own lives diminish during the past decades. On a wider level, low educational and health levels for women contribute significantly to an overall weakening of society. Economic reforms that actually dismantle the remnants of Pakistan's feudal rural economy need to be made to produce a society that functions to improve the condition of all its members.

CHAPTER SIX

The Way Ahead: Two Post-2015 Pakistani Scenarios

As international public attention paid to Afghanistan dwindles with the drawdown of international military forces, there is a risk that corresponding attention to the critical issues facing Central and South Asia will not be sustained.[1] While comparisons to the early 1990s disengagement from Afghanistan after the apparent victory over the Soviet Army are attractive, the two situations are not analogous. The United States and others in the international community will likely not lose focus on regional counterterrorism priorities. Yet, this is a thin basis on which to place the case for sustained engagement given the domestic unpopularity of the U.S.-led intervention after more than thirteen years.[2] There is a real fear that, unless policies are adjusted to accommodate changing realities on the ground, diplomatic disengagement could have a negative cascading effect on regional trend lines for stability and economic growth. Western aid and assistance projects in particular are likely to lose the urgency that ushered them in after the initial intervention in 2001 and with the 2009-10 surge of forces to Afghanistan. Nevertheless, this region must remain a principal interest of the international community.

In order to provide some clarity to the international community's approach to the way ahead, we analyze two possible scenarios for Pakistan's near term future. The first envisions an outwardly engaged Pakistan, sketching what its internal development and role in the region would look like under more optimal circumstances. This scenario envisions a brighter future for Pakistan, one in which it has tackled its extremism problem, increased the credibility and performance of its governance, improved several key economic indicators, and embarked on the beginnings of regional cooperation and a comprehensive and stability-enhancing security policy. It would also entail greater trade linkages (not only in the region), greater travel and tourism, academic and informational exchanges, and robust investment flows. This progress would be matched by a renewed commitment by the international community to working with Pakistanis on mutual priorities that represent a positive and constructive series of goals for the region. Admittedly ambitious, it provides a baseline for comparison and a target for the kind of change this report sees as critical to Pakistan's ability to meet the promises of its founders.

The second scenario attempts to forecast the repercussions of a continuation of the status quo by reflecting what would likely be a continued decline in security and economic benchmarks within Pakistan and a continued pattern of strained relations among nations in the region. It is instructive to consider the consequences of a policy path that looks very much like the one currently being followed for the three key sectors of security, economy, and governance.

It is critical to understand how each prospective path will have profound implications for the ways in which the United States, the international community, and Pakistan and its neighbors approach issues affecting regional progress. While the international community—NATO and, principally, the United States—is planning to transition away from the large-scale counterterror and nation-building mission inside Afghanistan that it has pursued for over a decade, this is not the end to challenges that drew it in at the end of 2001. Nor is there a sufficient level of appreciation in the wider international community as to how strategically crucial the region will remain, even absent a significant western military presence.[3]

Outwardly Engaged Pakistan

This Working Group believes that this region is poised to capitalize on cooperative management of the problems facing each country if the transitions of 2015 can be exploited fully for bold policy-making. If the challenges analyzed in this report can be managed, the outlook for the region will be significantly improved. There are myriad cross-border issues—security, economic, ecological—that can only be tackled if the countries of the region can be encouraged to increase efforts toward normalization that have proceeded sporadically and erratically since the late 1990s. The potential opportunities of a growing youth population and natural pathways for trade are too promising to not consider how best to realize regional cooperation on a wider and deeper scale than has so far been feasible.

Both scenarios should take as their starting point the important transitions taking place within Pakistan and the region. Recent years have already seen a series of important shifts that will determine developments within and beyond Pakistan. In 2013, Pakistan saw an important democratic transition as one civilian government peacefully passed power to another. While the government has promised action on several priorities, now nearly two years removed from its inauguration it is far from clear that they have the capacity to meet every priority. In addition to a change in civilian leadership, Pakistan in 2013 also saw a change-over in chief of army staff. Elections in India and Afghanistan last year signaled potentially significant changes in each country's outlook in its bilateral relationship with Pakistan and broader regional posture. President Ghani will still be fighting a war against members of the Taliban with more modest support from U.S. and NATO forces. Additionally, Prime Minister Modi will have to decide whether and how to approach the on-and-off normalization process that has been subject to the interference of not only violent non-state actors but powerful constituencies within each nation's political and security establishments.[4]

The region as a whole will experience for the first time in over a decade an Afghanistan without a large international presence. The economic changes of the previous twenty years mean that developing economies, particularly India and China, view their interests in the region through a different lens. Iran's isolation from the international community shows initial signs of some relaxing. How that may translate to a new approach to its eastern borders remains to be seen, but it is another factor that needs to be taken into consideration. Many interested nations see Pakistan as the crossroads connecting Russia and Central Asia, the Middle East, and South and East Asia. What has been under-analyzed are the requisite steps to realize and sustain that vision.

In the first scenario, both Pakistanis and internationals should take as their respective frames of reference an outwardly engaged Pakistan. This represents an idealized policy outcome and a best-case scenario that is nevertheless useful for projecting a hopeful end-result of a series of necessary and overdue policy steps. For too long, there has been a lack of coordination on policy-making on all sides. From the particulars of this path we will then be able to fashion recommendations to achieve that vision. In both foreign and domestic policy observers need to ask first what Pakistan can and should do for itself and second what the international community can do to facilitate those commitments.

Foreign Policy: Transition across the Region

For the last part of the Pervez Musharraf era through the Zardari government and since Nawaz Sharif took his oath as Prime Minister there has been a remarkable consistency in the Pakistani state's public narrative about the region it occupies. Officially and informally, especially with international interlocutors, Pakistani state authorities express a desire for regional cooperation starting with improved trade with India, friendship and increased trust with Afghanistan, enhanced ties with Iran, and the deepening of already strong relations with China. The most recent planning document, Vision 2025, presents regional connectivity as one of its seven priority areas. While this point is understood intellectually, its impact on actual policy development is muted, especially in the face of myriad domestic security threats. The base rationale for this impetus is the Pakistani state's increased awareness of the value of the country as a trade corridor for the region. There are obvious linkages between this value as a trade partner and the opportunity costs of allowing instability and insecurity to undermine business confidence. Pakistan's status as a potential corridor power has a flipside: it can be a conduit for transnational trade, but also for transnational militancy. It is for both reasons that sustained international engagement is necessary.

In an outwardly engaged scenario, Pakistan could serve as the catalyst and hinge for a new era of wider regional cooperation that takes as an opportunity the Western drawdown in Afghanistan. Such a project would require continued normalization of the various bilateral relationships in the region (including but not limited to Afghanistan-Pakistan, India-Pakistan, and the role Iran might play vis-à-vis both their immediate neighbors and the region as a whole). Such diplomatic and economic engagement is in the national interests of each country and also the international community as a whole. While Western nations have predominantly focused on the threat of transnational terrorist networks, this focus alone cannot productively sustain international engagement with the region in future years. Rather, it is past time to produce a vision of Pakistan that places that country in the appropriate context of the entire region. South Asia is regularly cited as one of the least economically integrated regions in the world.[5] That is a reality that is no longer sustainable given current population trends and the necessity of governments in the region to expand economic growth aggressively. Additionally, absent a serious effort in the region at greater cooperation and integration, it will be hard to sustain foreign support for Pakistan—especially among foreign audiences and particularly in fatigued Western capitals that perceive Pakistani motives as unsympathetic and even hostile.

In this scenario, the countries of the region would seize on initial steps toward growing cooperation. The current hesitant and stalled moves toward India-Pakistan normalization would be re-animated, starting with dialogue to de-escalate and prevent further clashes along the Line of Control. Military-to-military interactions would build confidence to allow further political discussions through the composite dialogue of the Foreign Ministries, but also on the prime ministerial level.[6] Such a dialogue could first address more obvious confidence-building possibilities such as Sir Creek, Wullar Barrage, and later even Siachen Glacier as a basis for further and more ambitious steps. Additionally, under such a scenario Pakistan would continue its stated support for an Afghan-led reconciliation process between the legitimately elected government in Kabul and those members of the Taliban willing to negotiate a possible end to their insurgency. India's interests in Afghanistan, long controversial to a Pakistan fearful of that country's assistance to the Karzai government, would not be subject to a Pakistani veto. However, continued discussions at the diplomatic and political level would encourage and reinforce the essentially economic and humanitarian focus of Indian assistance. Regardless of Pakistani objections, India would play a crucial role in trying to sustain post-2001 development gains in Afghanistan, which should be a priority for Pakistan as well. There is potentially more common ground between the two countries that needs to be discovered and developed.

The United States in this scenario could play an important role in fostering a counterterrorism dialogue on a regional basis. Starting with bilateral discussions on the ambassadorial level a structure could be constructed that would gradually include all of the countries in the region. The new leadership in both India and Afghanistan offers an opening for a fresh evaluation of counterterrorism strategies. In parallel, the United

States should move beyond a narrow focus on counterterrorism and bring to bear broader, more sophisticated approaches to Pakistan.

While the United States has often hailed the strategic nature of its bilateral relationship with Pakistan, such rhetoric must not promise more than either country can sustain. It is highly likely that current aid levels will be unsustainable.[7] If such a reassessment occurs, it is incumbent on the international community to target its aid at those projects and issues that will have the most positive impact and that can be administered effectively by the Pakistani state. To date, no comprehensive plan for aid programs to Pakistan exists among the international donor community. It should be an essential first step for the Pakistani government to collaborate with its bilateral aid and assistance partners and multilateral donor institutions to craft such a strategy. The long-term view of such an effort should be the full transition of Pakistan away from an aid economy to a globally integrated and productive economy based on a series of reforms in the fiscal and regulatory spheres as well as the inclusion of socially marginalized groups in the formal economy.

China: Pakistan's Only Friend?

In addition to the potential new roles played by India and the United States, other powers also have opportunities to shape the economic growth of the region. The role of China in this scenario will be crucial. If the United States and China can identify and act on a constructive agenda for economic relations among the nations in the region, it would go a long way to marginalizing those voices that still stand in the way of broad-based cooperation with Pakistan. While each nation will be guided by its own self-interest and the realities of geopolitics, there could be the beginning of a framework for better management of relations. China has, in addition to investment interests in Afghanistan and Pakistan, a desire to see stable regimes alongside its southwestern border. China has begun a series of trilateral discussions with a rotating group of interested nations, including Russia, Afghanistan, India, and Pakistan, looking at how to make political cooperation beyond counterterrorism concerns a reality.

There may be space for both the United States and China to build on these efforts. The latter's "all-weather" friendship with Pakistan is an oft-cited axiom of international relations in South Asia standing in contrast with the up-and-down nature of Pakistan-U.S. ties. China is Pakistan's largest trading partner accounting for about 17 percent of total trade according to 2012 figures.[8] It is instrumental in supplying Pakistan's military and collaborates on the expansion of its civilian nuclear power program. Not only could Pakistan enjoy fruitful bilateral relations with both China and the United States, but these relationships could also facilitate a better working relationship between China and the United States.

As the internal situation within Pakistan deteriorates, however, it is an open question whether the Chinese will reassess the current nature of the relationship. China's pursuit of its national interests is quite calculating and the official relationship will be on good standing only so far as Pakistan can provide utility. China will not support Pakistan unconditionally if its interests are compromised by Pakistani institutional deficiencies, especially in addressing the extremism challenge. Pakistan cannot serve as a political and strategic adjunct for China if it is paralyzed by internal militancy, poor governance, an anemic economy, and provides a sanctuary for transnational militant groups that target countries abroad, including China. Whether Chinese pressure on Pakistani leadership to pursue reform either alone or in concert with other concerned powers is enough to spur dedicated action is a question that will animate future discussions about the country.

No amount of political cooperation will solve all of the myriad problems facing the region. There are some, including Afghan and Pakistani Taliban elements, who will remain unreconciled to any inclusive political order in South and Central Asia to say nothing of friendly economic relations between traditional rivals. Yet, a broadly cooperative environment will position each nation in the region to better weather tensions arising from the actions of spoilers.

Trade Relations

An outwardly engaged Pakistan would be well positioned as a transit point for wider regional trade and economic cooperation.[9] By taking advantage of its new trade relationships, Pakistan would be better positioned to provide opportunities for its people, two-thirds of whom are under age 30.[10] Under this scenario, a gradual relaxation of tensions allows the region as a whole to follow through on several initiatives and ideas that have been floated in recent years since the Lahore Declaration in 1998. The first step would be a finalization of Most Favored Nation status (or a similar approach[11]) between India and Pakistan. Preferential tariff treatment is insufficient on its own unless it is followed up by measures to increase market access and reduce non-tariff barriers. Additionally, there are opportunities for a build-up of border crossing infrastructure. For too long, commerce and people-to-people movement have been hindered by under-investment in such facilities due often to legitimate security concerns but also to the inertia of the long-stalled normalization process.[12] The process would likely not be a speedy one, but it is a necessary condition for realizing gains from further relaxation of tensions. A liberalized visa regime and accelerated foreign direct investment would optimally lead to the improvement of cross-border transit links expanding the current underdeveloped methods of moving goods across the border.[13]

Macroeconomic/Fiscal Stability

Stabilizing Pakistan's economy is an essential next step to ensuring the long-term prospects of security and governance; just as security provides space for economic growth good governance ensures its sustainability. Prime Minister Sharif campaigned on a platform of economic growth with particular focus paid to improving Pakistan's infrastructure (the PML-N's election manifesto was entitled "Strong Economy-Strong Pakistan").[14] Righting the economic ship involves addressing both energy and fiscal challenges, which have so far eluded the efforts of successive Pakistani governments. It also involves an expansion of participation in the formal economy.

In 2013, the World Bank published an exhaustive report on putting Pakistan on a path to aggressive but sustainable job growth.[15] Not only does it need more jobs for a growing population, those jobs need to be of a higher quality—permanent and well paying. Additionally, the report acknowledged that the economic gains Pakistan currently enjoys accrue to the top strata of society, a circumstance that needs to be addressed. With very little income redistribution from rich to poor through government policy, any improvement in the lower and middle classes must come through economic growth in the country at large where the poor are disproportionately susceptible to downturns.

The World Bank report targets a 7 percent growth rate goal; an ambitious metric reflective of structural reforms and improvement in governance, especially changes that allow for an increase in hitherto crowded out private sector investment.[16] Among the measures the Bank highlighted as potentially the most effective, several are approachable through a cooperative framework: cutting electricity load-shedding by a half (roughly back to 2007 levels), bringing Pakistan's fiscal deficit to a sustainable level, building foreign reserves, raising private sector credit, export diversification, increased tax revenue, reducing the burden of certain business regulations, civil service reform, raising infrastructure spending to 5 percent of GDP, overhauling state-owned enterprises (including privatization where appropriate), reforming the construction sector, increasing agricultural activity, and improving technical and vocational instruction.[17]

That is an extensive and ambitious list; it would be necessary under this scenario for Pakistan and its partners in the international community to prioritize those areas that are both achievable in the current political atmosphere and that will have the largest economic impact. Under an idealized outwardly engaged scenario, these efforts would be at the cornerstone of efforts to restore Pakistan to a positive growth trajectory, a development that will also raise economic indicators for a region that would under the same scenario be growing closer together.

The benefits of such aggressive, high quality growth are clear, according to the World Bank's analysis:

- 2.1 percentage point gain in private consumption,
- 7.6 percentage point drop in unemployment,
- 9.9 percentage point of GDP decline in government debt, and
- 5.5 percentage point decline in the headcount poverty rate.[18]

One sector to pursue in this scenario is further trade liberalization outside of the South Asia region. In December 2013, the European Union extended duty-free market access to Pakistani goods. In order to support the economic growth of Pakistan, its other partners and principally the United States should follow up the European Union's Generalised Scheme of Preferences Plus (GSP+) move by addressing their own barriers to trade.[19] Pakistani government officials have long asked for tariff reductions and removal of non-tariff barriers to help their enterprises compete against other textile-producing countries. However, these measures have always met opposition in the U.S. Congress and by organized labor, whose members are fearful that more international cooperation will harm industries and jobs. Nevertheless, just as priority has been given to broad trade agreements with East Asia as part of the Obama administration's "pivot," consideration should be given to how Pakistan fits into that framework as long as it is accompanied by a realization that tariff reduction would only be a first step.

An improved economic scenario in which gross domestic product growth is rising steadily year-on-year and in which the government is collecting more revenue and delivering electricity to its businesses will go part of the way to reversing declining confidence in Pakistani governance. Expanding trade ties with western nations and those within the immediate region would be a first step in this scenario. Concurrently there would be a serious strategy to tackle Pakistan's energy woes and develop a comprehensive development strategy.

Solving the problems of the energy sector has long been identified as a key first step in correcting Pakistan's economic problems. Not only does the importation of expensive fossil fuels drain Pakistan's financial resources, but also the daily load-shedding interrupts commerce and industry throughout the country. In the outwardly engaged scenario, Pakistan would stabilize the circular debt issue that has undermined the fiscal health of the entire energy sector and reform the utility companies involved in the production and transmission of power (including strengthening mechanisms for the collection of tariffs). Far too many members of Pakistan's upper strata get away with not paying their bills.

In the longer-term, Pakistan's energy strategy must focus on creating access to affordable energy for the broad majority of its population. The volatility of fossil fuel prices, especially given the global need to address climate change, suggests that the bulk of the solution may have to come from elsewhere. The country needs a strategy that can address the enormous current shortfall and also be sustainable over the longer-term.

Progress on trade issues is dependent on progress on the several foreign policy priorities previously noted. The economic growth trajectories of Pakistan should not be expected to improve (or even to continue at present rates) without a normalization of Pakistan's regional relations. Not only will a less-tense neighborhood facilitate the day-to-day operation of cross-border trade, but confidence-building in an ideal scenario would eventually lead to a reduction in the budgetary space afforded to military expenditure, an arena in which South Asia is one of the fastest-growing regions.[20] The ultimate goal would be the gradual shift from a Pakistan reliant on foreign aid and economic assistance (including ad hoc emergency assistance from individual nations) to one that can generate needed revenue from robust trade.[21]

Domestic Policy

The inherent tension between Pakistan's foreign and domestic policies has been complex and shifting. The improvement of one both depends on and reinforces the other. If nations in the region want to realize a vision for wider cooperation, several of Pakistan's domestic priorities need to be addressed. By shoring up the capabilities of Pakistan's democratic order it will add credibility to the advances in representative governance that have been made over the past six years. An essential longer-term goal and a prerequisite for enhancing Pakistan's democratic order remains effective leadership of civilians in defining and executing foreign and security policies. Unfortunately, the domestic challenges facing Pakistan are numerous and varied. Consequently, prioritization is necessary to guide decision-making by representatives of the international community and by Pakistanis themselves.

Acknowledging the corrosive effects of anti-state religious extremism would be a necessary adjunct to any military or law enforcement action against groups like the TTP. There is still space to argue for a more vigorous defense of the values of Pakistan's constitution—ones that are shared by the international community at large. For many years, segments of Pakistani society have been under siege by a constellation of violent non-state actors who have targeted religious minorities, political and religious liberals, and various organs of the state, especially military and law enforcement officials from senior generals to ordinary policemen. If an outwardly engaged Pakistan is to be realized, Pakistani society needs to come to grips with the problems inherent in rising extremism. While the nascent peace process collapsed in the face of militant attacks and then the beginning of an offensive into North Waziristan, the path ahead remains murky, especially with the threat of retaliation in Pakistan's cities and the existence of non-TTP aligned groups that have also visited violence on ordinary Pakistanis.

The cornerstone of such an effort would be a comprehensive national counterterrorism strategy embraced by the government and military and blessed by a reasonable cross-section of the opposition parties. With violent extremism no longer confined to its frontiers, but deeply embedded in cities such as Karachi, a unified plan is needed now more than ever. After the Peshawar school attack, the military offensive underway in North Waziristan has now been expanded, at least in theory, nationwide.

The National Plan of Action announced by Prime Minister Sharif is certainly a comprehensive list that if fully funded and implemented would constitute a robust and holistic counterterrorism effort—but remains unclear how capable and committed the country's leaders truly are to the program beyond a revival of the death penalty. Perhaps even more importantly, the capabilities of Pakistan's law enforcement agencies and judicial processes are incapable of meeting the challenge of the National Plan of Action—a fact that necessitated the adoption of the Twenty-First Amendment to the constitution and the establishment of military courts and will require further and sustained efforts to build institutional capacity.

This discussion is clearly meant to represent an ideal scenario of Pakistan's potential dependent on a series of policy choices that would be difficult to design and pursue under the best of circumstances. The purpose is to provide all concerned Pakistanis—and their supporters in the international community—with a future template for relations, taking into consideration the positive policy outcomes for the wider South Asian region in a way that has not been previously well articulated.

Pakistan on a Glide Path toward Failure

Alongside the positive scenario there should be a realization of the downside risks if Pakistan cannot address its well-known security, economic, and governance deficiencies. The alternative scenario is deeply worrying. It is worth exploring at length, since it represents what is now at stake in the region. This scenario attempts to forecast the repercussions of a continuation of the status quo by reflecting what would likely be a continued decline in security and economic performance within Pakistan and a continued pattern of strained relations among nations in the region. The United States is in the initial stages of a strategic reassessment directed to the shifting of resources and attention to East Asia. However, such a transition should take into account the potential risks of what might happen to the South Asia region in a status quo or declining scenario. There is more at stake for the United States and the international community beyond the role of the Taliban and the status of the central leadership of al Qaeda.

In this scenario, the current negative trends will continue to impact the trajectory of Pakistan's progress, limiting and overwhelming the country's ability to capitalize on any of the previously identified positive trends. A continued paralysis of governance combined with present economic and security challenges would have profound negative implications. While some international observers may engage in strategic *schadenfreude* that the compromises and contradictions of Pakistan's security and foreign policies have hobbled it, the damage within Pakistan and without would be harrowing and continued engagement would have a serious moral dynamic behind it.

Foreign Policy

A scenario that assumes a continuation or even deterioration in the status quo would have obvious negative repercussions for regional security and diplomatic relations. Absent further policy action, the tensions in the region will persist, which represents a dangerous trend for the immediate future and a threat to positive changes in Afghanistan. Instead of being well situated as a nexus for cross-border trade, Pakistan would continue to struggle in normalizing its bilateral relationships with Afghanistan and India. This scenario would posit a Pakistan that will continue to feel the need to play a double game in Afghanistan with support and guidance to anti-government elements in anticipation of potentially similar moves by Iran, India, and Russia. These elements would operate in a different environment from the one existing after the 2001 intervention. Pakistan has no desire for the Taliban to take control in Afghanistan, but its military and intelligence arms are still attracted to using them as leverage. There is a new nexus that further draws together militants on both sides of the Afghanistan-Pakistan border, as well as sectarian groups operating solely within Pakistan.

The inability of Pakistan to tackle violent non-state actors who have long-standing connections to elements in the military and intelligence agencies will impact its future relations with India, Afghanistan, the United States, and the rest of the international community. If there continues to be a permissive environment for such groups, Pakistan's government will not enjoy a monopoly over the making and execution of its own foreign policy. Rather, any initiatives toward normalization with either India or Afghanistan will be subject to a veto by armed groups exercised in part through violence against Pakistanis.

Pakistan's relations with the international community beyond the region would also suffer under a status quo scenario. There would be very little appetite among Western legislatures to continue assistance programs absent necessary policy shifts. Such an effort at disengagement would be a disservice to ordinary Pakistanis whose prospects would be undermined by the alienation of the international community. Those very few who would step in to replace that funding are likely to do no better at advancing best practices in governance. Even China, which has been noticeably consistent in maintaining a close official relationship that embraces "non-interference and peaceful economic collaboration," will need to reconsider the extent of its support.[22] Chinese investment cannot succeed in an atmosphere of pervasive insecurity and at the hazard of China's own security interests.

Macroeconomic/Fiscal Stability

A continuingly underperforming Pakistani economy would harm not only this generation of Pakistanis, but future generations as well. Without immediate policy remedies, the low economic growth and high inflation currently plaguing Pakistan's economy will likely continue. Such an under-performing trajectory will rob Pakistan's youth, one of the world's largest, of their full potential. According to the World Bank's recent country economic memorandum, Pakistan's labor force is projected to grow by 3.5 percent a year in the aggregate with 1.5 million young workers entering the force every year. Continuing trends in female participation would add to those numbers.[23] If the entire economic picture remains as discouraging as it is now, those new entrants into Pakistan's job market will be limited in their opportunities.

A Pakistan that cannot achieve strong growth will have cascading negative effects for the region as well. Economic growth fueled by trade and other cross-border interactions would be sacrificed. Negative development indicators for the region at large would undermine progress that has already been made in combating abject poverty. In this alternative and pessimistic scenario, the faltering energy sector would continue to plague Pakistan's economy, which would see the flight of business-minded elites who can no longer run profitable enterprises within Pakistan. An accelerated "brain drain" of talent with access to capital would further erode not only Pakistan's economic outlook, but also threaten its ability to manage its dwindling foreign reserves. The resulting negative impact where the government sees further erosions of the tax base as well as flexibility in the budget might hamper crucial improvement of the education sector, producing further frustration in coming generations.

Domestic Policy

In a deteriorating scenario, we should expect a continued disconnect between elite decision-makers and the population at large. A continuing leadership crisis where most of the electorate are losing or have lost trust in the traditional parties could further give strength to fringe elements, including ultra-nationalist and Islamist movements whose interests would diverge even further from the international community's.

Unfortunately for the stability of Pakistan, the loss of confidence in the government will likely fuel the advance of terror attacks from groups such as the TTP, especially if it splinters further. It is likely that the present government would not be able to follow up the current offensive with the governance measures necessary to avoid a repeat of situations where terrorists can congregate and operate openly on Pakistani soil.

The need to adopt a hedging strategy, one in which the international community focuses less on building a partnership with Pakistan and more on containing the damage from events beyond its control, cannot be ruled out. Instead of a constructive partnership, the international community led by the United States has legitimate concerns about the spread of transnational terrorism and may feel it necessary to create security assistance programs for both India and Afghanistan to ensure that those nations can meet threats, including from Pakistan; a course of action that could exacerbate the very security dilemma that gives space to the operations of some of these groups in the first place. Further, a lack of improvement on security-related threats will ensure a limited and flawed future external engagement that continues to view Pakistan exclusively through the lens of counterterrorism policy.

Moving toward the Outwardly Engaged Scenario

Knowing the best-case scenario is only a first step. It is essential to think through and sequence the longer-term policies necessary to arrive there. Not only must these policies be realistic to the international community whose funding priorities will be in flux, but they must be credible to Pakistanis as well. For far too long, recommendations for international engagement in Pakistan have been divorced from the perspectives of the country's citizens, especially outside of elite circles. Western disengagement from the region will only fuel the long-held perceptions that the United States is transactional in its approach to Pakistan and only interested in the region when its specific interests are at stake rather than trying to take into account how those in the region might envision their own interests.

Defining Pakistan's primary national interests will require an appreciation for the prospects offered by an aggressive agenda for realizing further regional integration. Pakistan's pursuit of such a goal would bring benefits from normalization with India as well as an improvement in the bilateral relationship with Afghanistan. The entire region has hitherto failed to unlock its potential as a hub for transit and trade, especially in energy and with respect to links with Iran and Central Asia. Adding to these untapped advantages is the spur to economic growth arising from a growing youth population that could help exploit new cross-border economic connections.

What should be the strategic vision of the international community for South Asia? This vision follows from the discussion of what Pakistanis themselves want. Once there is a clear appreciation for that concept the international community can proceed on more realistic ground. Just as India's future is increasingly interdependent with Southeast Asia and China, so it could also be interdependent with Pakistan, Afghanistan, and Central and West Asia. This could be the basis for a regional strategic vision that integrates Pakistan as part of a long-term strategy to achieve goals rather than solely as a tactical response to threats.

This Working Group believes that despite the difficulties in Pakistan's relationships with its neighbors and tension with members of the international community, the deteriorating Pakistan scenario with its potential for an acceleration of negative trends is an unacceptable policy outcome—for Pakistanis, their neighbors, and anyone interested in peace and stability of the region as a whole.

CHAPTER SEVEN

Recommendations of the Working Group

Recommendations for the International Community

Regional Diplomacy

Afghanistan

- The United States and the international community should use diplomatic, intelligence, and military channels to promote a "negative symmetry deal" on militant proxies, whereby Afghan authorities cease any support or guidance to anti-Pakistan militants inside Afghanistan and, conversely, Pakistan commits similarly to end support for anti-Afghan insurgent elements.
- The United States and Pakistan need to engage in sustained dialogue on Afghanistan, distinct from other bilateral issues.
- The infrastructure investments envisioned under the Chinese-Pakistan Economic Corridor should be widened in due course to include Afghanistan and India.
- The United States, the European Union, and other nations should continue to promote India-Pakistan dialogue in their future relations with Pakistan.

Counterterrorism

- Develop the prospects for regular, high-level counterterrorism cooperation between and among the United States, the European Union, other interested states, and Pakistan to include intelligence sharing, discussion of technology transfer, and establishing guidelines for future Pakistani indigenous armed drones and how that might relate to a more transparent future joint U.S.-Pakistan program, including closer cooperation on targeting.

- Promote U.S. and multilateral cooperation, training, and exchanges with Pakistani law enforcement and national security agencies.
- Explore a regional basis for counterterrorism, including Indo-Pakistani bilateral cooperation and Indo-Chinese dialogue on counterterrorism, and multilateral efforts through the Shanghai Cooperation Organization focused specifically on intelligence sharing and law enforcement cooperation. Specific opportunities for coordination with China should be aggressively pursued.

Encouraging India and Pakistan Military Confidence-Building Measures

- To reduce uncertainty around the deployment of conventional military forces by India and Pakistan and to deal with issues of potential surprise, the international community should consider outlining for both sides a program for the exchange of military missions that will have the right to travel in and will be invited to maneuvers on the other side.
- To reduce the possibility of an accidental use of nuclear weapons and to assuage concerns about the need for confidence-building measures on the deployment of nuclear and conventional arms by both sides, the international community should press both India and Pakistan to ensure full de-mating of warheads and delivery vehicles, stationing weapons further from frontiers, improving civil control in Pakistan over weapons release, strengthening of existing permissive action links (PALs), and where possible developing new technologies to prevent accidental, insurgent, or criminal capacity to acquire and use nuclear weapons.
- Encourage both sides to follow up the unilateral moratoria on testing by engaging more deeply in talks to discuss the creation of bilateral instruments to limit, monitor, and verify an end to testing.
- Encourage both sides jointly to set limits on overall warhead and nuclear delivery vehicle production.
- Encourage India and Pakistan to include the institution of joint inspections of nuclear facilities in both countries as part of a

renewed bilateral dialogue. Third-party technical and other monitoring, including by the United Nations, should be considered for deployment to provide each side with real-time assurances about the posture and disposition of military forces on each side (conventional and nuclear).

- Bilateral progress on nuclear issues between India and Pakistan should eventually be expanded with a parallel effort with China to engage in steps to avoid further expansion of nuclear armaments in South Asia.

Sino-American Cooperation

- The United States and China should elevate Pakistan-related discussions to a top-tier issue in their bilateral engagement, including adding a Deputy Minister-level meeting focused on South Asia. Such steps should reinforce engagement on mutual interest in a stable and inter-connected South Asia.
- Deepen such a dialogue process over time to encompass India, Iran, and Afghanistan.

International Regionalization of Bureaucratic Policy Framework

- To advance properly a more integrated approach to the region, states involved in the region should erase artificial geographical divisions within their relevant diplomatic, development, and security ministries.
- The U.S. military should consider Pakistan and India as part of the same theater (Combatant Command) for U.S. military purposes, paralleling consolidation in the National Security Council and State Department.

International Commitment to Constitutional Authority

- The international community, which has previously expressed its unreserved support for the democratic process in Pakistan, should reinforce this message in all interactions with Pakistani officials, specifically conveying a policy of "no support" for unconstitutional changes of government. These discussions should also reflect that democratic systems require internal accountability.

Economic Relations

Trade

- The international community should encourage India and Pakistan to finalize the nearly negotiated 2014 framework for preferential trade access (Most Favored Nation status). Both sides need to extend trade talks into the area of non-tariff barriers (Pakistan is fortunate in having one of the fastest-growing export markets at its doorstep).

- As a first step toward broader trade liberalization, the United States should follow the European Union's lead in being an open market for Pakistani textiles, including assurances on international labor and environmental standards.

- Both the European Union and the United States should identify a future roadmap for extending free trade policies to India and Pakistan, perhaps as a potential extension of the Trans-Pacific Partnership (TPP) (The European Union's extension of GSP+ is instructive here).

- The United States should encourage the expansion of bilateral interactions by non-governmental and business organizations.

Energy

- The international community, especially the United States, the European Union, and China, with the cooperation of multilateral institutions such as the World Bank and Asian Development Bank, should create a Power South Asia initiative to ensure affordable energy access for the region. The initiative should prioritize the energy trade measures under way between India and Pakistan, expanding them to other nations in the region, including connections with Central Asia, with the ultimate long-term goal bringing about a regionally integrated energy market with wide grid connectivity.

- The United States, conditioned on the continued success of the P5+1/Iran negotiating process and as part of a winding down of sanctions on Iran, should drop the prohibition on supply of hydrocarbons to Pakistan and India through pipelines from Iran and Turkmenistan via Iran. The purpose is to assure that the possibility of receiving greater supply that way is opened up to both countries.

- As a long-term step toward the greening of Pakistan's fuel mix, the international community should prioritize support for renewable energy, including facilitating financing options.

International Assistance

- Aid and assistance agencies should work with donor governments to coordinate a narrower range of development programs within Pakistan: disaster management (including water management), education, and health. International development assistance organizations should work closely with relevant Pakistani ministries to avoid duplication of efforts where particular agencies have comparative advantages in certain regions or on specific issues, and to increase monitoring of discrete aid programs. International assistance should encourage improvements in rule of law and accountability.
- Organizers of international assistance programs should support the Pakistani government's multi-year roadmap that, while reflecting the immediate needs of Pakistan, takes as its goal the eventual end of large aid programs.
- The United States and others should seek to involve Gulf states and other Muslim-majority countries financially in a major support package for education in Pakistan.

Recommendations for the Government of Pakistan

Regional Diplomacy

Afghanistan

- Pakistan should support the new unity Afghan government in its efforts at a dialogue with the Afghan Taliban on reconciliation, including facilitating the direct participation of Afghan Taliban members sheltering in Pakistan who are willing to look at an end to violence and participation in the political process.
- Pakistan and Afghanistan should open a dialogue on outstanding issues beginning with a move on cooperative border management.
- In this dialogue, Afghanistan and Pakistan should adopt urgent measures to address the safe havens utilized by insurgencies on

their respective borders. The principles underlying such a dialogue ought to include:

» Pakistani government messaging toward the Afghan Taliban and Pakistani public, including a public explanation of how Afghan negotiation efforts with the Afghan Taliban need to be matched by Pakistani efforts such as cessation of support for the Afghan Taliban and Haqqani network actions against Afghan targets.

» Pakistan's cessation of support to the Afghan Taliban as part of a negative symmetry deal with Afghanistan whereby it ceases support for Pakistani Taliban elements sheltering in Afghanistan.

- The joint dialogue should transition to consider the economic dimensions of the relationship, including addressing future prospects for transit trade with India and China.

- The long-term goal of such a dialogue would be to move to where Afghanistan and Pakistan could begin discussions of a strategic partnership agreement.

- India and Pakistan have shared interests in a stable Afghanistan, and a joint dialogue along those lines should be pursued, addressing Indian economic assistance and Pakistani recognition of and relations with the legitimate government in Kabul.

Counterterrorism

- Arresting the scourge of violent extremism requires a holistic effort by Pakistani authorities to implement in full Prime Minster Sharif's declaration that no distinction will be made between "good" Taliban and "bad" Taliban. This approach must necessarily extend to all non-state actors that threaten violence both within and beyond Pakistan. The National Action Plan (NAP) is a welcome articulation of national will to fight terrorism, which must be matched by dedication of resources to the military as well as to Pakistan's internal civilian law enforcement agencies and judiciary, which are also at the front of the fight.

- While the current military offensive unfolds, Pakistan needs to develop a framework for principles of engagement and potential reconciliation with TTP factions willing to pursue non-violence. The main issues underpinning a deal would be no concession on the part of the Pakistani government regarding territorial control or supremacy of the constitution. Respect for the fundamental rights of women and other marginalized groups must be a prerequisite for such an effort. A deal should be founded on the principle that violence must end in favor of participation by the TTP, or factions thereof, in democratic processes and political activities. Beyond that, a discussion on redlines regarding sheltering of foreign militants, and the role of Pakistan's federal government in determining the legal status of FATA would be required.

Normalization of the FATA

- Acknowledging that the offensive against the TTP cannot succeed without addressing the feelings of alienation among residents of FATA, the Pakistani government should pursue incremental reforms to normalize FATA's legal status, including the identification of the necessary and appropriate administrative infrastructure.
- While the exact methodology of normalization should be flexible, the end state should be the maturation of the seven Agencies into seven districts, whether as part of Khyber Pakhtunkhwa or as a separate province. Of special importance to this process is the expansion of the justice and law enforcement infrastructure, which suffers from an absence of police and regular courts.

Civil-military relations

- The leadership of elected civilians in defining and executing Pakistani national security strategy is the central instrument for the formulation and implementation of a Pakistani foreign policy that can take advantage of the many regional opportunities available to Pakistan. Pakistan's maturing democratic traditions must over time address questions about the accountability of all publicly-funded organizations to elected leaders.
- The supremacy of civilian policy leadership over the military needs to be reasserted through the work of the Cabinet Committee on National Security and the National Security Division, which should be provided with the personnel, leadership, and resources to address security threats.
- The degree of parliamentary oversight over defense issues should be enhanced and all decisions involving the use of national military power should be taken by an accountable, elected prime minister.

India & Kashmir

- The current dialogue to de-escalate and prevent armed clashes along the Line of Control needs to be pursued as a diplomatic priority.
- Enhanced mechanisms for mutual confidence-building between the military in Pakistan and their counterparts in India should be instituted: including more regular usage of hotlines, more effective pre-notification of military exercises in proximity to the border regardless of size, and non-intrusion into airspace accords for sensitive areas (Siachen glacier).
- In efforts to deepen the discussion and as confidence-building measures unfold to restore the relationship it may be possible to accelerate the dialogue toward a discussion on Kashmir based on the following principles:
  » Pakistan, India, and the people of Jammu and Kashmir are the three negotiating parties (others can constructively play a role through quiet bilateral contacts with all parties).
  » Discussions should include the rights of Kashmiris to decide their internal affairs.
  » Kashmir should be de-militarized with law and order issues handled by Kashmir itself (repeal of the Armed Forces Special Powers Act). Indian forces should be withdrawn and Pakistan should give a full commitment not to send fighters or weapons of any kind into Kashmir.
  » Kashmir should be able to trade freely across Pakistan and India.

Economic Relations and Governance

Trade and Transport

- There is a need to shift toward export-promotion—including supportive fiscal and monetary policies, export capacity-building, quality enhancement, reliable energy access for exporters, strengthening of trade missions, and aggressive pursuit of growing export markets, especially China, India, and the Middle East, as well as more traditional markets, such as the United States, the European Union, and Japan.
- Create a modern customs regime with trained and well-compensated officials and up-to-date technology. Previous agreements to

liberalize the India-Pakistan visa regime should be implemented on a fast-tracked basis.

- Identify prospects for joint Indo-Pakistani projects to improve border infrastructure, including improving rail and well as road links. Congestion at crossing points and the lack of investment reduce benefits for even the existing limited trade. This should be a priority for U.S. assistance from the Enhanced Partnership with Pakistan Act of 2009 (Kerry-Lugar-Berman).
- Extend the Afghanistan-Pakistan Transit Trade Agreement to India. Pakistan should permit trucks from Afghanistan to cross borders in the western direction with Indian goods. Prioritize U.S. New Silk Road links through the improvement of the road infrastructure serving Afghanistan, China, India, and Iran. Expand pre-existing links between the two Punjabs. Explore customs pre-clearance in Lahore and Amritsar for sealed shipments.

Energy

- Pakistan needs to develop an aggressive and strategic energy policy that can meet immediate needs in an affordable manner as well as ensure long-term sustainability of energy availability. The short-run options include overcoming the political and logistical obstacles to the import of affordable hydrocarbons from Iran and Central Asia, exploiting local hydrocarbon resources, and enhancing the efficiency and transparency of energy supplies. Longer-term options will have to focus inevitably on renewable energy mainly by seeking support for lowering their costs and gaining access to the relevant technologies. Both options will have to be underpinned by aggressive governance reforms of the sector to ensure modernization and maintenance of existing energy resources and to implement long awaited reforms that ensure cost-recovery.
- Pakistan and India should also each be assured of additional energy access beyond Iran and Turkmenistan with the ultimate aim of an efficient regional energy market, including capacity for imported Liquefied Natural Gas, and free oil and natural gas trade.
- Seek to connect the electrical grids in the region for full effectiveness. Develop and incorporate in an environmentally respectful manner hydropower in Myanmar and Nepal. There is precedent here in grid connections between India and Bangladesh. Seek

connectivity with Central Asia and Iran as well in mating with ongoing and planned projects.

- Taking as a starting point the draft Memorandum of Understanding for importation of power from India, develop a short-term roadmap for the finalization of open India-Pakistan electricity trade with external multilateral financing directed toward the upgrading of critical grid infrastructure.

Economic Management

- Pakistan needs to set an ambitious goal of accelerating its rate of growth to levels comparable with its neighboring countries in South Asia. This will require a focus on four areas: curbing population growth, enhancing energy access, improving governance, and promoting exports.
- Population policy has been sidelined under pressure from fundamentalist elements for too long. It is clear now that the country will not be able to make serious progress until population growth is brought down significantly. The government needs to face up to this challenge and pursue it with commitment and dedication.
- The Prime Minister's Office working with the Council on Common Interests should provide the resources to enable the achievement of the Vision 2025 proposals. The commission should engage high-level Pakistani and international economic thinkers as a standing body to advise the prime minister and minister of finance.
- The Prime Minister's Office and the Council of Common Interests should translate the Planning Commission's goal of reaching high-income status by 2047 into a detailed roadmap to be implemented vigorously that includes metrics for cutting load-shedding, lowering deficits, and increasing tax revenue (see next section).
- The governance reform goals of Vision 2025 should identify methods for eliminating corruption, including conflict of interest, increasing transparency, overhaul of procurement policies, and a robust freedom of information law.
- Existing regulatory bodies should be reformed to reinforce their autonomy and independent decision-making authority. The authority for anti-corruption efforts should be a blend of executive and parliamentary authority with transparent and time-bound guidelines for the open initiation and completion of cases.

Tax Revenue

- No other progress on Pakistan's economic problems can be expected to gain traction without a serious effort to compel the paying of tax, especially by Pakistani elites, and the overall expansion of the tax base.

Education

- Work with Muslim and non-Western nations with advanced primary and secondary school systems—Malaysia, Singapore, South Korea—to partner with Pakistani schools on best practices and funding mechanisms with the eventual goal of completely indigenous funding of Pakistani primary and secondary education.
- Develop a revised general curriculum in which major skills are taught and in which more advanced grades receive greater access to modern and utilitarian subjects. The curriculum should be designed to foster analytical skills, tolerance, mutual understanding, and equality among Pakistan's constituent ethnic and religious groups.
- Universities from the developed countries should be encouraged to expand further projects and partnerships in Pakistan.
- Fulfill the promise to spend at least 4 percent of the GDP on education in order to meet the demands of the National Plan of Action for Education presented by Prime Minister Sharif to the United Nations General Assembly side session on education in September 2013. This will help address the enrollment of millions of out of school children, especially girls.

Agriculture

- In the 1960s, Pakistan was able to benefit from the Green Revolution because of sustained investment in agriculture and agricultural institutions—with active support from the United States. As the challenges confronting the agriculture sector have transformed, the country needs to invest in a new phase of agricultural development oriented to water efficiency, climate proofing, ecological conservation, and social and gender equity.
- Seek to develop programs for larger ownership by current renters of small plots, increased irrigation, expansion of micro finance, and more modern farming techniques such as drought-proof and saline-resistant seeds.

- Rationalize the collection of taxes at the federal and provincial level by transferring collection of provincial agricultural taxes from the provincial administration to the Federal Bureau of Revenue, which will be rebated to the provinces. Seek to create an agriculture investment fund fed by land taxes to provide financing for projects to improve agricultural efficiency.

Provincial Relations

- The holding of local government elections, the legislation for which has been tabled, needs to be a priority across all of Pakistan's provinces.
- Provincial authorities should be encouraged to institute further model development programs in health and education.

Securing Fundamental Human and Civil Rights

- Advancement of equal citizenship and protection of religious sects should be encouraged by all provinces as a natural outgrowth of the values which are of critical importance to the successful prosecution of a comprehensive counterterrorism strategy.
- Law enforcement accountability must be strengthened if ordinary Pakistanis are expected to have any faith in the exercise of their justice system.
- The government should make the prevention of violence against women a priority, including enforcement of existing laws and revision of Pakistan's criminal procedure code, along with regular provincial review of statistics to gauge performance.
- Official accountability for forced disappearances in Balochistan should be pursued, beginning with a discussion of potential compensation.

Notes

Chapter 1

1. Daniel Markey, "No Surprises in Pakistan" *Indian Express*, April 2, 2014, http://indianexpress.com/article/opinion/columns/no-surprises-in-pakistan/99/, accessed April 2, 2014.

2. Paul Krugman, *The Age of Diminished Expectations: U.S. Economic Policy in the 1990* (Cambridge, Massachusetts: MIT Press, 1997), 11.

3. Yaroslav Trofimov, "In Its Own War on Terror, Pakistan Piles Up Heavy Losses," *Wall Street Journal*, March 10, 2014, http://online.wsj.com/news/articles/SB10001424052702304691904579348820227129270, accessed March 13, 2014.

4. Syed Raza Hassan, "Pakistan's Hindus, other minorities face surge of violence," *Reuters*, May 5, 2014, http://www.reuters.com/article/2014/05/05/us-pakistan-minorities-idUSBREA440SU20140505, accessed May 5, 2014.

5. Huma Yusuf, "Minorities Report," *New York Times*, December 6, 2012, http://latitude.blogs.nytimes.com/2012/12/06/ahmadis-a-special-target-of-discrimination-in-pakistan/, accessed September 17, 2014.

6. Bhagwandas, "Sindh records 421 cases of violence against women in three months," *Dawn*, October 11, 2014, http://www.dawn.com/news/1137148, accessed February 27, 2015.

7. British Council, "Next Generation Goes to the Ballot Box," http://www.nextgeneration.com.pk/next-generation-goes-to-the-ballot-box/index.php, accessed March 13, 2014.

8. Farhan Bokhari and Victor Mallet, "Pakistan Taliban leaders pledge allegiance to Isis," *Financial Times*, October 14, 2014, http://www.ft.com/intl/cms/s/0/cfdc723c-53b1-11e4-929b-00144feab7de.html#axzz3PTbPBpGW, accessed January 6, 2015.

9. Munawer Azeem, "Police to act against Jamia Hafsa over Daish video," *Dawn*, January 9, 2015, http://www.dawn.com/news/1155803, accessed January 19, 2015.

10. When chief of army staff general Raheel Sharif visited Beijing in early June 2014, he met with Chinese officials, who expressed their concern about both infiltration of anti-Chinese terrorists in Xinjiang province from Pakistan and the safety of Chinese workers in Pakistan. Meng Jianzhu, who oversees security operations in Xinjiang, offered to enhance counterterror cooperation. "China ask Gen Sharif to set up crackdown against militants," *Pakistan Today*, June 6, 2014, http://www.pakistantoday.com.pk/2014/06/06/foreign/china-asks-gen-sharif-to-step-up-crackdown-against-militants/, accessed June 6, 2014.

11. Ministry of Planning, Development, and Reform, "Pakistan 2025: One Nation-One Vision," August 2014, http://pakistan2025.org/wp-content/uploads/2014/08/Pakistan-Vision-2025.pdf, accessed February 27, 2015.

12. All of these initiatives have generated varying responses, but there is obviously limited enthusiasm among traditional elements of the security establishment, as well as Kashmir-centric political actors, especially those with terrorist credentials.

13. This new rigid tone was first seen after Modi's inauguration, when the Indian government protested the meeting between Pakistan's High Commissioner and the Hurriyat Conference, a coalition of Kashmiri separatist leaders. Ellen Barry, "India Cancels Talks after Pakistani Envoy Meets with Separatists," *New York Times*, August 18, 2014, http://www.nytimes.com/2014/08/19/world/asia/india-cancels-talks-after-pakistani-envoy-meets-with-separatists.html?_r=0, accessed August 18, 2014.

14. Ananth Krishnan, "Corridor of Uncertainty," *India Today*, April 15, 2015, http://indiatoday.intoday.in/story/china-pakistan-kashmir-beijing-economic-corridor/1/427045.html, accessed April 8, 2015.

15. R. L. W. and L. P, "Measuring the arms merchants," *The Economist,* March 18, 2014, http://www.economist.com/blogs/graphicdetail/2014/03/daily-chart-13, accessed August 26, 2014; Farhan Bokhari and Charles Clover, "Pakistan nears deal to buy 8 Chinese submarines," *Financial Times*, April 1, 2015, http://www.ft.com/intl/cms/s/0/a2c22012-d845-11e4-ba53-00144feab7de.html#axzz3Weavhk9h, accessed April 7, 2015.

16. Provincial apex committees are the province-level mechanisms for coordination between military and civilian leaderships in implementing the National Action Plan. "Provincial Apex committees formed to implement NAP," *The News*, January 3, 2015, http://www.thenews.com.pk/article-170670-Provincial-Apex-committees-formed-to-implement-NAP, accessed January 20, 2015.

17. "America's Global Image Remains More Positive than China's: But Many See China Becoming World's Leading Power," Survey, Pew Research Center, July 18, 2013, http://www.pewglobal.org/2013/07/18/americas-global-image-remains-more-positive-than-chinas/.

18. The clearest formulation of this ideal is represented in a speech Jinnah gave in August 1947, days before Pakistan's creation as an independent state: "You are free. You are free to go to your temples, you are free to go to your mosques or to any other place of worship in this state of Pakistan. You may belong to any

religion or caste or creed—that has nothing to do with the business of the state." Quoted in Shahzeb Jillani, "The search for Jinnah's vision of Pakistan," BBC News, September 11, 2013, http://www.bbc.com/news/world-asia-24034873.

Chapter 2

1. Jon Boone, "Taliban militants arrested over attack on Pakistan school that left 130 dead," *Guardian*, January 14, 2015, http://www.theguardian.com/world/2015/jan/14/taliban-militants-attack-pakistan-arrests, accessed January 14, 2015.

2. *Afghanistan: Negotiating Peace: The Report of The Century Foundation International Task Force on Afgahnistan in Its Regional and Multilateral Dimensions* (New York: Century Foundation Press, 2011).

3. "GSP Plus: EU grants duty-free market access to Pakistani goods," *Express Tribune* December 12, 2013, http://tribune.com.pk/story/644585/gsp-plus-eu-grants-duty-free-access-to-pakistani-goods/, accessed December 12, 2013.

4. Dean Nelson, "India election 2014: Narendra Modi says India and Pakistan should be allies in war on poverty," *Daily Telegraph*, May 6, 2014, http://www.telegraph.co.uk/news/worldnews/asia/india/10810421/India-election-2014-Narendra-Modi-says-India-and-Pakistan-should-be-allies-in-war-on-poverty.html, accessed May 6, 2014.

5. Niharika Mandhana, "On Kashmir Visit, India's Modi Takes a Swipe at Pakistan," *Wall Street Journal*, August 12, 2014, http://blogs.wsj.com/indiarealtime/2014/08/12/on-kashmir-visit-indias-modi-takes-a-swipe-at-pakistan/, accessed August 12, 2014.

6. Nisha Taneja, "Enhancing India-Pakistan Trade," *New America Foundation*, January 2013, http://security.newamerica.net/publications/policy/enhancing_india_pakistan_trade, accessed May 14, 2014.

Chapter 3

1. Shahbaz Rana, "Economic survey: 13-year war on terror cost $102.5 billion," *Express Tribune*, June 2, 2014, http://tribune.com.pk/story/716558/economic-survey-13-year-war-on-terror-cost-102-5-billion/, accessed April 2, 2015.

2. The Indian perception that Pakistan is dragging its feet on the prosecution of the Mumbai terrorists remains a serious issue in the attempt to improve bilateral relations. Likewise, Pakistan complains about lack of information-sharing regarding the investigation of the Samjhota Express.

3. "No discrimination between 'good' and 'bad' Taliban," *Express Tribune*, December 17, 2014, http://tribune.com.pk/story/808258/no-discrimination-between-good-and-bad-taliban-pm-nawaz/, accessed December 17, 2014.

4. South Asian Terrorism Portal, "Fatalities in Pakistan Region Wise: 2014," http://www.satp.org/satporgtp/countries/pakistan/database/fatilities_regionwise2014.htm, accessed January 4, 2015.

5. Umer Nangiana, "Report indicates drastic increase in sectarian violence in 2012," *Express Tribune,* January 6, 2013 http://www.nextgeneration.com.pk/next-generation-goes-to-the-ballot-box/index.php, accessed March 13, 2014.

6. "HRCP's concern as Jan–July figures show sharp rise in Karachi killings," Human Rights Commission of Pakistan, July 15, 2013, http://hrcp-web.org/hrcp-web/hrcps-concern-as-jan-july-figures-show-sharp-rise-in-karachi-killings/, accessed March 4, 2014.

7. Tim Craig, "Airstrikes targeting Pakistan Taliban continue in response to school massacre," *Washington Post,* December 20, 2014, http://www.washington post.com/world/airstrikes-targeting-pakistan-taliban-continues-in-response-to-school-massacre/2014/12/20/fc2527dc-8825-11e4-9534-f79a23c40e6c_story.html, accessed January 5, 2015.

8. Jack Serle, "Pakistan drone strike pause is the longest of Obama's presidency," *The Bureau of Investigative Journalism,* February 18, 2014, http://www.thebureauinvestigates.com/2014/02/18/pakistan-drone-strike-pause-is-the-longest-of-obama-presidency/, accessed March 15, 2014.

9. Karen DeYoung and Greg Miller, "U.S. said to curtail drone strikes in Pakistan as officials there seek peace talks with Taliban," *Washington Post,* February 4, 2014, http://www.washingtonpost.com/world/national-security/us-curtails-drone-strikes-in-pakistan-as-officials-there-seek-peace-talks-with-taliban/2014/02/04/1d63f52a-8dd8-11e3-833c-33098f9e5267_story.html?hpid=z1, accessed February 4, 2014; "TTP Shura, govt committee to come face-to-face on Tuesday," *Express Tribune,* March 24, 2014, http://tribune.com.pk/story/686674/peace-talks-to-be-held-on-tuesday-at-secret-location/, accessed March 24, 2014.

10. Mehreen Zahra-Malik and Haji Mujtaba, "Drones hit Taliban hideouts in 'joint Pakistan-U.S.' raid, say officials," Reuters, June 12, 2014, http://www.reuters.com/article/2014/06/12/us-pakistan-drones-idUSKBN0EN0TP20140612?feed Type=RSS&feedName=worldNews, accessed June 12, 2014.

Chapter 4

1. Y. Hijioka, E. Lin, J. J. Pereira, R. T. Corlett, X. Cui, G. E. Insarov, R. D. Lasco, E. Lindgren, and A. Surjan, "Asia," in: *Climate Change 2014: Impacts, Adaptation, and Vulnerability. Part B: Regional Aspects. Contribution of Working Group II to the Fifth Assessment Report of the Intergovernmental Panel on Climate Change,* ed. V. R. Barros, et al. (Cambridge, U.K.: Cambridge University Press, 2014), 1327–70, https://www.ipcc.ch/pdf/assessment-report/ar5/wg2/WGIIAR5-Chap24_FINAL.pdf, accessed April 6, 2015.

2. Mehmet Burk, "The Next Black Swan: Rapid Changes in Context," The Center for Climate and Security, February 25, 2014, http://climateandsecurity.org/2014/02/25/the-next-black-swan-rapid-changes-in-context/, accessed February 25, 2014.

3. Tim McDonnell, "Explained in 90 seconds: Breaking the carbon budget," *Grist,* November 24, 2013, http://grist.org/climate-energy/explained-in-90-seconds-breaking-the-carbon-budget/, accessed January 5, 2014.

4. Rory Medcalf, "India Poll 2013: Facing the Future: Indian views of the world ahead," Lowy Institute for International Policy, http://www.aii.unimelb.edu.au/sites/default/files/India%20Poll%202013.pdf, accessed March 10, 2014.

5. Khadija Zaheer and Anna Colom, "Pakistan: How the people of Pakistan live with climate change and what communication can do," Climate Asia, http://downloads.bbc.co.uk/rmhttp/mediaaction/pdf/climateasia/reports/Climate Asia_PakistanReport.pdf, accessed March 5, 2014. The data was collected through both household survey and qualitative focus group discussions held from March 2012 to January 2013.

6. Zaheer and Colom, "Pakistan: How the people of Pakistan live with climate change," 18.

7. Of the people surveyed, 14 percent were either very confident or quite confident in the federal government; 17 percent for provincial and local governments. Half of those surveyed were confident in the ability of their neighborhoods to take action. Ibid., 22.

8. Ferya Ilyas, "PM Nawaz announces Rs1B aid package for Tharparkar," *Express Tribune*, March 10, 2014, http://tribune.com.pk/story/681057/pm-nawaz-announces-rs1b-aid-package-for-tharparkar/, accessed March 10, 2014.

9. Safiya Aftab, "Pakistan's energy crisis: causes, consequences, and remedies" *Norwegian Peacebuilding Resource Centre*, Expert Analysis, January 2014, http://www.peacebuilding.no/Regions/Asia/Pakistan/Publications/Pakistan-s-energy-crisis-causes-consequences-and-possible-remedies.

10. Ahmad Fraz Khan, "12-hour power cuts are back" *Dawn*, March 10, 2014 http://www.dawn.com/news/1091967/12-hour-power-cuts-are-back, accessed March 10, 2014.

11. Aftab, "Pakistan's energy crisis."

12. "Joint Statement by President Obama and Prime Minister Nawaz Sharif," The White House, October 23, 2013, http://www.whitehouse.gov/the-press-office/2013/10/23/joint-statement-president-obama-and-prime-minister-nawaz-sharif.

13. Aftab, "Pakistan's energy crisis."

14. Amir Wasim, "Gas reserves sufficient only for 16 years, NA told," *Dawn*, March 6, 2014, http://www.dawn.com/news/1091350/gas-reserves-sufficient-only-for-16-years-na-told.

15. "Power board approves projects of 2,630MW capacity," *Express Tribune*, March 6, 2014, http://tribune.com.pk/story/679362/power-board-approves-projects-of-2630mw-capacity/.

16. Ari Phillips, "Pakistan's First Solar Project Is One of the World's Largest," ThinkProgress, May 13, 2014, http://thinkprogress.org/climate/2014/05/13/3437021/pakistan-inaugurates-first-solar-park/, accessed May 13, 2014.

17. Aamir Saeed, "Sun Shines on Union between Solar Power and Electric Grid in Pakistan," Reuters, January 6, 2015, http://www.scientificamerican.com/article/sun-shines-on-union-between-solar-power-and-electric-grid-in-pakistan/, accessed January 7, 2015.

18. Sandeep Dikshit, "India, U.S. energy talks today," *The Hindu,* March 10, 2014, http://www.thehindu.com/news/national/india-us-energy-talks-today/article5767602.ece, accessed March 10, 2014.

19. Simon Rogers and Mona Chalabi, "UN peacekeeping missions: who provides the most troops," *The Guardian,* April 30, 2013, http://www.theguardian.com/news/datablog/interactive/2013/apr/30/un-peacekeeping-missions-mapped?CMP=twt_gu, accessed February 23, 2014.

Chapter 5

1. Additionally, the report revealed that no one in Pakistan has been prosecuted for tax fraud in the past twenty-five years. House of Commons, International Development Committee, "Pakistan," March 26, 2013, http://www.publications.parliament.uk/pa/cm201213/cmselect/cmintdev/725/725.pdf, accessed January 20, 2015.

2. The $2 billion was viewed as a great success, exceeding initial expectations of $500 million. Kazim Aslam, "Pakistan raises $2 billion through Eurobonds," *Express Tribune,* April 9, 2014, http://tribune.com.pk/story/693308/pakistan-raises-2-billion-through-eurobonds/, accessed September 22, 2014.

3. Shahbaz Rana, "Power tariff: Govt misses IMF deadline, loan tranche in jeopardy," *Express Tribune,* September 12, 2014, http://tribune.com.pk/story/761084/power-tariff-govt-misses-imf-deadline-loan-tranche-in-jeopardy/, accessed September 12, 2014; International Monetary Fund, "IMF Executive Board Completes Fourth and Fifth Reviews under Extended Fund Facility Arrangement for Pakistan, and Approves US $1.05 Billion Disbursement," Press Release No. 14/583, December 17, 2014.

4. "Pakistan," Transparency International, http://www.transparency.org/country#PAK, accessed September 10, 2014.

5. World Economic Forum Competitiveness Rankings, http://reports.weforum.org/global-competitiveness-report-2014-2015/rankings/, accessed September 17, 2014.

6. United Nations Development Programme, Human Development Index, http://hdr.undp.org/en/content/table-1-human-development-index-and-its-components, accessed September 17, 2014.

7. Reporters without Borders, World Press Freedom Index 2014, http://rsf.org/index2014/en-index2014.php, accessed September 17, 2014.

8. "Educational attainment and employment outcomes," Paper commissioned for the Education for All (EFA) Global Monitoring Report 2013/4, UNESCO, 2013, http://unesdoc.unesco.org/images/0022/002263/226333e.pdf, accessed June 30, 2014.

9. "Punjab government will educate street children," *The Nation,* June 22, 2014, http://www.nation.com.pk/national/22-Jun-2014/punjab-government-will-educate-street-children, accessed July 14, 2014.

10. "KPK approves education reforms package," *The Nation,* August 4, 2013, http://www.nation.com.pk/national/04-Aug-2013/kpk-approves-education-reforms-package, accessed July 1, 2014.

11. "Public spending on education, total (% of GDP)," The World Bank World Development Indicators Database, http://data.worldbank.org/indicator/SE.XPD. TOTL.GD.ZS, accessed July 14, 2014.

12. "Demand for education and skills building in Pakistan," ICEF Monitor, April 8, 2014, http://monitor.icef.com/2014/04/demand-for-education-and-skills-building-in-pakistan/, accessed July 14, 2014.

13. "Pakistan Social and Living Standards Measurement Survey (PSLM) 2012-13 Provincial/District," Pakistan Bureau of Statistics, April 2014, http://www.pbs.gov.pk/content/pakistan-social-and-living-standards-measurement-survey-pslm-2012-13-provincial-district, accessed 14 July 2014.

14. Ministry of Education, Training, and Standards in Higher Education, "National Plan of Action 2013–2016: Achieving Universal Primary Education in Pakistan," August 2013, http://educationenvoy.org/wp-content/uploads/2013/07/National-Plan-of-Action_Pakistan1.pdf, accessed April 22, 2015.

15. PSLM 2012–13 Provincial District.

16. S. Hyder, "The elixir that is the youth," *Aurora Magazine* (July/August 2013), http://aurora.dawn.com/2013/07/03/the-elixir-that-is-the-youth/, accessed July 14, 2014.

17. Durr Nayab, "Demographic Dividend or Demographic Threat in Pakistan," Pakistan Institute for Development Economics, December 4, 2006, http://www.pide.org.pk/pdf/Seminar/Demographic%20Dividend.pdf, accessed July 14, 2014.

18. "Pakistan: Demographic and Health Survey, 2012–13," National Institute of Population Studies Islamabad, Pakistan, December 2013, https://dhsprogram.com/pubs/pdf/FR290/FR290.pdf.

19. Don Rassler, C. Christine Fair, Anirban Ghosh, Arif Jamal, Nadia Shoeb, "The Fighters of Lashkar-e-Taiba: Recruitment, Training, Deployment and Death," Occasional Paper, Combating Terrorism Center at West Point, 2013, http://explore.georgetown.edu/publications/index.cfm?Action=View&DocumentID=70803, accessed February 27, 2015.

20. C. Christine Fair, "Insights from a Database of Lashkar-e-Taiba and Hizb-ul-Mujahideen Militants," *Journal of Strategic Studies* (2013), http://dx.doi.org/10.1080/01402390.2013.811647, accessed October 22, 2013.

21. "Internet users (per 100 people)," World Bank, http://data.worldbank.org/indicator/IT.NET.USER.P2, accessed July 14, 2014.

22. Aroosa Shaukat, "Being imaginative: PITB compiling games to make learning fun," July 3, 2014,http://tribune.com.pk/story/730463/being-imaginative-pitb-compiling-games-to-make-learning-fun/.

23. Bytes for All, "Hate Speech: A Study of Pakistan's Cyberspace," June 2014, http://content.bytesforall.pk/sites/default/files/Pakistan_Hate_Speech_Report_2014.pdf, accessed April 7, 2015.

24. Inter-Parliamentary Union, "Women in national parliaments," February 1, 2015, http://www.ipu.org/wmn-e/classif.htm, accessed April 7, 2015.

Chapter 6

1. Recent reports have indicated that the United States is considering slowing the pace of the troop withdrawal. David Lerman, "Pentagon Chief Tells Afghan Leaders He'll Reasses U.S. Exit," Bloomberg, February 20, 2015, http://www.bloomberg.com/news/articles/2015-02-21/new-pentagon-chief-visits-afghanistan-as-troop-options-reviewed, accessed February 27, 2015.

2. Tal Kopan, "Poll: The most unpopular U.S. war," *Politico*, December 30, 2013, http://www.politico.com/story/2013/12/afghanistan-war-unpopularity-poll-101596.html. Eighty-two percent of those polled opposed the conflict, compared to 69 percent disapproval for the Iraq war at its height, and 60 percent for the war in Vietnam.

3. Despite its combined population of over 1 billion people, neither India nor Pakistan was mentioned in President Obama's 2014 State of the Union Address. Barack Obama, "2014 State of the Union Address," http://www.washingtonpost.com/politics/full-text-of-obamas-2014-state-of-the-union-address/2014/01/28/e0c93358-887f-11e3-a5bd-844629433ba3_story.html.

4. Prime Minister Narendra Modi invited Prime Minister Nawaz Sharif to Delhi for his inauguration. While the meeting was described as cordial, Modi did warn that the Pakistani government must do more to cease attacks by militants located in Pakistan against India. Sanjeev Miglani and Shyamantha Asokan, "India's Modi prods Pakistan on terror on first days as PM," Reuters, May 27, 2014, http://www.reuters.com/article/2014/05/27/us-india-politics-idUSKBN0E70ST20140527, accessed May 27, 2014. Further statements have referenced the need for clashes between Pakistani and Indian military units along the Line of Control to cease before the process could proceed.

5. The World Bank cites the figure that intra-regional trade is just five percent of total trade, as compared to 25 percent for the Association of Southeast Asian Nations (ASEAN). "Regional Integration in South Asia," World Bank, March 24, 2014, http://www.worldbank.org/en/region/sar/brief/south-asia-regional-integration, accessed May 14, 2014.

6. On his trip to Narendra Modi's inauguration, Sharif said he was open to restarting the composite dialogue. "Mother's love drives diplomacy: Sharif sari for PM Mom," *The Times of India*, June 6, 2014, http://timesofindia.indiatimes.com/india/Mothers-love-drives-diplomacy-Sharif-sari-for-PM-mom/articleshow/36120241.cms, accessed June 6, 2014.

7. In particular, the Coalition Support Funds, by which the United States reimburses Pakistan for ensuring the safety of NATO convoys transiting between Karachi and Afghanistan.

8. "Trade in goods with Pakistan," European Commission Directorate-General for Trade, http://trade.ec.europa.eu/doclib/docs/2006/september/tradoc_113431.pdf, accessed March 4, 2014.

9. Fahd Humayun, "Looking Beyond India's Chabahar Option," Jinnah Institute, February 13, 2014, http://jinnah-institute.org/looking-beyond-indias-chabahar-option/, accessed February 13, 2014.

10. Michael Kugelman, "Pakistan's Demographics: Possibilities, Perils, and Prescriptions," in *Reaping the Dividend: Overcoming Pakistan's Demographic Challenges*, ed. Michael Kugelman and Robert M. Hathaway (Washington, D.C.: Woodrow Wilson International Center for Scholars, December 2010), http://www.wilsoncenter.org/sites/default/files/ReapingtheDividendFINAL.pdf, 6.

11. 12. Tridivesh Singh Maini, "Opening up the Munabao-Khokrapar crossing," *The Hindu*, June 12, 2014, http://www.thehindu.com/opinion/op-ed/opening-up-the-munabaokhokhrapar-crossing/article6105073.ece?homepage=true, accessed June 12, 2014.

13. "A comprehensive and integrated international land transport policy needs to be put in place, not only to provide rail and road services to connect the two countries but also to service other countries by linking seaports through land borders." Nisha Taneja, "Enhancing India-Pakistan Trade," New America Foundation, January 2013, http://security.newamerica.net/publications/policy/enhancing_india_pakistan_trade, 2014, 17.

14. "PMLN Manifesto: English," PML-N Website, April 18, 2013, http://www.pmln.org/pmln-manifesto-english/, accessed February 24, 2014.

15. The World Bank, "Pakistan: Finding the Path to Job-Enhancing Growth: A Country Economic Memorandum" August 5, 2013, http://documents.worldbank.org/curated/en/2013/08/18124048/pakistan-finding-path-job-enhancing-growth-country-economic-memorandum, accessed March 10, 2014.

16. "In contrast, swiftly raising annual GDP growth to 7 percent assumes that broad and sustained structural reforms would improve the investment climate, economic governance, and private investment in physical and human capital. It also assumes a minimum rise in total investment from 14 percent of GDP to 18 percent (with a 70–30 split between private and public investment) support by higher private and government savings—and a rise in annual total factor productivity growth from 1–2 percent to 3–4 percent per year." Ibid., 13.

17. Ibid., 15–19.

18. Ibid., 13.

19. The plus denotes additional duty free exports for developing world countries. "GSP Plus: EU grants duty-free market access to Pakistani goods," December 12, 2013, http://tribune.com.pk/story/644585/gsp-plus-eu-grants-duty-free-access-to-pakistani-goods/, accessed January 5, 2014.

20. Trefor Moss, "More Money, More Power for Asian Militaries," *Wall Street Journal*, February 5, 2014, http://blogs.wsj.com/searealtime/2014/02/05/more-money-more-power-for-asian-militaries/, accessed May 14, 2014.

21. "Pakistan," Organisation for Economic Co-operation and Development, February 24, 2014, http://www.oecd.org/dac/stats/documentupload/pak.jpg, accessed March 5, 2014.

22. Imtiaz Gul, "What China wants," *The Friday Times*, March 21, 2014, http://www.thefridaytimes.com/tft/what-china-wants/, accessed March 21, 2014.

23. World Bank, "Pakistan: Finding the Path to Job-Enhancing Growth," 9.

About the Members
of the Working Group

Thomas R. Pickering, *Chair,* is vice chairman of Hills and Company, an international consulting firm providing advice to U.S. businesses on investment, trade, and risk assessment issues abroad, particularly in emerging market economies. He retired in 2006 as senior vice president, international relations for Boeing. He has had a career spanning five decades as a U.S. diplomat, serving as under secretary for political affairs, ambassador to the United Nations, to Russia, India, Israel, Nigeria, Jordan, and El Salvador. He also served on assignments in Zanzibar and Dar es Salaam, Tanzania. He holds the personal rank of career ambassador, the highest in the U.S. Foreign Service.

Tariq Banuri is a professor in the Departments of Economics and City and Metropolitan Planning at the University of Utah, where he also serves as senior adviser to the Sustainability Office and the Office of Global Engagement. He served most recently as the director of the United Nations Division for Sustainable Development. He was a coordinating lead author on the Nobel Prize-winning Intergovernmental Panel on Climate Change (IPCC). Before joining the United Nations, he was senior fellow and director of the Future Sustainability Program at the Stockholm Environment Institute. He was the founding executive director of the Sustainable Development Policy Institute (SDPI), a Pakistani think tank. He received his PhD in economics from Harvard University.

Richard Barrett is a senior vice president at The Soufan Group and a former British diplomat and intelligence officer who formerly headed the United Nations al Qaeda and Taliban Sanctions Monitoring Team. Before being appointed to head the Sanctions Monitoring Team, he worked for the British government in the Security Service (MI5), the Foreign Office, and the Secret Intelligence Service (MI6). He was director of Global Counter Terrorism Operations both before and after the attacks on September 11, 2001, in the United States. Among other things, he is a board member of the International Centre for Counter-Terrorism in The Hague; the Transnational Crisis Project in London; the Global Center on Cooperative Security in Washington, D.C.; the Center for Research and Security Studies in Islamabad, the Global Community Engagement and Resilience Fund in Geneva, the Oxford Research Group in the United Kingdom, PS21 (Project for the Study of the 21st Century) in Washington and London, and the Center for the Study of United Nations Systems and the Global Legal Order in New York. He is a fellow of the New America Foundation, Washington, and of the Royal United Services Institute, London, and a founding director of a Master's Program in Financial Integrity at Brown University in Providence, Rhode Island.

Hikmet Çetin was the NATO senior civilian representative (SCR) for Afghanistan (2004–06). He was elected to the Turkish Parliament in 1977 as a member of the Republican People's Party (CHP). He has served as the deputy prime minister, minister of foreign affairs, and speaker of the Turkish Grand National Assembly.

Steve Coll is dean and Henry R. Luce Professor of Journalism at the Columbia University Graduate School of Journalism. He is a staff writer at *The New Yorker*, the author of seven books of nonfiction, and a two-time winner of the Pulitzer Prize. Between 1985 and 2005, he was a reporter, foreign correspondent, and senior editor at the *Washington Post,* where he served as managing editor between 1998 and 2004. He is the author of *Ghost Wars: The Secret History of the CIA, Afghanistan, and Bin Laden, from the Soviet Invasion to September 10, 2001,* published in 2004, for which he received an Overseas Press Club Award and a Pulitzer Prize. His 2008 book *The Bin Ladens: An Arabian Family in the American Century* won the PEN/John Kenneth Galbraith Award for Nonfiction in 2009 and was a finalist for the Pulitzer Prize for biography. His most recent book is *Private Empire: ExxonMobil and American Power* which won the *Financial Times*/Goldman Sachs Award as the best business book of 2012. He served as president of the New America Foundation, a public policy institute in Washington, D.C., between 2007 and 2012. He graduated from Occidental College in Los Angeles in 1980 with a degree in English and history.

Robert P. Finn, *Principal Investigator,* was the first U.S. ambassador to Afghanistan in more than twenty years, from March 22, 2002, until November 27, 2003. He was a professor in Turkic studies and international relations at Princeton University for ten years, and is currently a non-resident fellow of the Liechtenstein Institute on Self-Determination at Princeton. From 2012 until 2014, he was a visiting scholar at Columbia University. He was a member of the Foreign Service (1978–2005). In 1992, he opened (as chargé d'affaires) the U.S. Embassy to Azerbaijan and served as chargé and deputy chief of mission for three years. He also served as the U.S. ambassador to Tajikistan (1998–2001) and had postings in in Turkey, Croatia, and Pakistan.

Antje Grawe most recently served as counselor for economic cooperation and head of development at the German Embassy in Pakistan. Her experience in Afghanistan and Pakistan spans over a decade. She was previously head of analysis and planning for the Office of the Special Representative of the Secretary-General (SRSG) for Afghanistan. She also served as political adviser to the head of mission of the European Union's Police Mission (EUPOL) in Afghanistan. She graduated with degrees in political science and history from the University of Trier, Institut d'Etudes Politiques in Bordeaux, France, and Uniwersytet Warszwski in Warsaw, Poland.

Jean-Marie Guéhenno is the president of the International Crisis Group. He previously was the Arnold Saltzman Professor of Professional Practice at Columbia University and the director of its center for international conflict resolution at the School of International and Public Affairs. He is also a non-resident senior fellow at the Brookings Institution. In 2012, he was appointed deputy joint special envoy of the United Nations and the Arab League for Syria. He left that position to chair the commission appointed by President François Hollande to review the French Defense and national security posture. Between 2000 and 2008, he served as the United Nations' under secretary-general for peacekeeping operations. A former French diplomat, he held the position of chairman of the *Institut des Hautes Études de Défense Nationale* between 1998 and 2000, and served as director of the French policy planning staff and as ambassador to the Western European Union.

Imtiaz Gul is the executive director of Center for Research and Security Studies (CRSS) that he founded in December 2007 with the support of Germany's Heinrich Boell Stiftung. The center is a research and advocacy outfit, focused primarily on security, rule of law, radicalization, and governance. He is a leading Pakistani expert on security, terrorism and radicalization issues, and has acted as a consultant to many national and foreign governmental and nongovernmental missions. Gul is the author of: *Pakistan: The Pivot for Hezbut Tahrir's Global Caliphate; Pakistan: Before and After Osama bin Laden; The Most Dangerous Place—Pakistan's Lawless Frontier; Al-Qaeda Connection—Taliban and Terror in Tribal Areas;* and *The Unholy Nexus; Pak-Afghan relations under the Taliban.*

Michael Wahid Hanna, *Principal Investigator,* is a senior fellow at The Century Foundation. He works on issues of international security, international law, and U.S. foreign policy in the Middle East and South Asia. He served as a co-director of The Century Foundation's International Task Force on Afghanistan, co-chaired by Ambassador Thomas R. Pickering and Ambassador Lakhdar Brahimi. He has published widely on U.S. foreign policy in newspapers and journals, including articles in the *New York Times,* the *Los Angeles Times,* the *Boston Globe, Christian Science Monitor,* the *New Republic, Democracy, Middle East Report,* and *World Policy Journal,* among other publications, and is a frequent contributor to *Foreign Policy.* He appears regularly on MSNBC, CNN, PBS, BBC, and NPR, including appearances on the *Charlie Rose Show* and *PBS NewsHour.* He served as a consultant for Human Rights Watch in Baghdad in 2008. Prior to joining The Century Foundation, he was a senior fellow at the International Human Rights Law Institute. From 1999 to 2004, he practiced corporate law with the New York law firm Cleary, Gottlieb, Steen & Hamilton. Fluent in Arabic, he was a Fulbright Scholar at Cairo University. He received a J.D. from New York University School of Law, where he was an editor of the *Law Review.* He is a member of the International Institute for Strategic Studies and was a term-member of the Council on Foreign Relations.

Ishrat Husain is dean and director of the Institute of Business Administration (IBA) in Karachi. He served as the chairman, National Commission for Government Reforms from 2006 to 2008. He previously served as the governor of Pakistan's Central Bank. He worked for the World Bank for over two decades. He is currently a member of Middle East Advisory Group of the IMF, the Regional Advisory Group of the UNDP, and was chairman World Economic Forum Global Advisory Council on Pakistan until June 2014. During 2009–10 he was appointed chair of the Pay and Pension Commission. From 2011–14 he served as an independent director on the board of Benazir Income Support Programme (BISP), the largest social safety net and conditional cash transfer program in Pakistan. He is currently convener, Economic Advisory Council, Ministry of Finance, and member, Advisory Council to the Minister of Planning, Development and Reforms. He is the author of *Pakistan: The Economy of the Elitist State*. He is the Distinguished National Professor of Economics and Public Policy at IBA and serves on the boards of several research institutes and philanthropic and cultural organizations. He obtained master's degree in development economics from Williams College and doctorate in economics from Boston University in 1978.

Asma Jahangir is a lawyer, advocate of the Supreme Court of Pakistan, and chairperson of the Human Rights Commission of Pakistan. From 2004 to 2010, she was the United Nations special rapporteur on freedom of religion or belief. Previously, she served as the United Nations special rapporteur on extrajudicial, arbitrary, and summary executions. In 2010, she became the first-ever female president of the Supreme Court Bar Association of Pakistan. She was instrumental in the formation of the Punjab Women Lawyers Association (PWLA) and the Women Action Forum (WAF). She is the author of two books, *Divine Sanction? The Hudood Ordinance* and *Children of a Lesser God: Child Prisoners of Pakistan*. She is the recipient of numerous international awards, including the American Bar Association International Human Rights Award; Millennium Peace Prize (2001); and UNESCO/Bilbao Prize for the Promotion of a Culture of Human Rights (2010).

Riaz Khokhar is a private consultant and senior fellow at the China-Pakistan Joint Think Tank at the National University of Science and Technology (Islamabad). He served as Pakistan's foreign secretary from

2002 to 2005. A career diplomat, he has been ambassador to the People's Republic of China and Mongolia, to the United States and Jamaica, and Bangladesh and Bhutan. He has also served as Pakistan's high commissioner to India from 1992 to 1997. He has previously served as a foreign policy and defense aide to Pakistani prime ministers Nawaz Sharif, Mustafa Jatoi, Benazir Bhutto, and Zulfikar Ali Bhutto.

Tariq Khosa until recently served as adviser to the United Nations Office on Drugs and Crime (UNODC) on Rule of Law and Criminal Justice in Pakistan. He retired from police service as federal secretary, Narcotics Control Division, in January 2011. He was director general, Federal Investigation Agency, in 2009, where he supervised investigations into the Mumbai terror attacks and also initiated a criminal investigation of the assassination of former Prime Minister Benazir Bhutto. His previous appointments include director general, National Police Bureau, in the Ministry of Interior; secretary of National Public Safety Commission, an oversight body of all the federal police departments; and the police chief of Balochistan Province. He graduated from the National Defence College, completing his master's degree in defence and strategic studies in 2004–05. After joining the Police Service of Pakistan in 1976, he served as assistant superintendent and superintendent of police in Punjab Province as well as in the Federal Investigation Agency and the National Police Academy. He was a Hubert Humphrey Fellow under the Fulbright Exchange Program at the Graduate School of Public Affairs, University of Washington (Seattle). After completing his master's degree in English literature from Government College Lahore (Punjab University) in 1972, he joined the Provincial Civil Service and served as a magistrate at Lahore from 1973 to 1975.

Jugnu Mohsin is the publisher of *The Friday Times*, a Lahore-based English-language independent newsweekly, where she is also the author of a monthly satire column. She is the recipient of the Committee to Protect Journalists' International Press Freedom award. She was also awarded the Sitara-e-Imtiaz by the Government of Pakistan. She is the host of a popular show on GEO television, *Jugnu*. She is a community organiser and trustee of the Mohsin Trust, which provides education, health care and hygiene support, and craft development in Okara, rural Punjab.

Cameron Munter is a retired career diplomat who served as America's ambassador to Pakistan from October 2010 until July 2012. Prior to his appointment as ambassador, he served in several capacities in Baghdad, Iraq, overseeing U.S. civilian and military cooperation in planning the drawdown of U.S. troops and establishing the first-ever provincial reconstruction team in Mosul. His past positions include U.S. ambassador to Serbia, where he negotiated Serbian domestic consensus for European integration while managing the Kosovo independence crisis, and deputy chief of mission at the U.S. embassies in the Czech Republic and Poland, where he managed the American contribution to those countries' integration into Western civilian and military institutions. He was also a director at the National Security Council under Presidents Bill Clinton and George W. Bush, executive assistant to the counselor of the State Department, and chief of staff of the NATO Enlargement Ratification Office at the State Department, in addition to serving other diplomatic assignments in Washington and overseas. His is currently professor of practice in international relations at Pomona College.

Ahmed Rashid is a well-known writer and commentator on Pakistan, Afghanistan, Central Asia, and the Middle East. He is the author of five books, including the best-selling *Taliban* and *Descent into Chaos: The U.S. and the Disaster in Afghanistan, Pakistan and Central Asia*. Other titles include *Jihad* and *The Resurgence of Central Asia* and, most recently, *Pakistan on the Brink, The Future of America, Pakistan, and Afghanistan*. His books have been translated into over forty languages and they have won numerous prizes. He writes regularly for the *Financial Times*, the *New York Times*, the *New York Review of Books*, Spain's *El Mundo*, BBC Online, and several Pakistani publications. *Foreign Policy* magazine chose him as one of the world's most important 100 Global Thinkers in 2009 and 2010. He serves on the board of New York's Committee to Protect Journalist, he is an adviser to Human Rights Watch, and he has also served on the board of advisers for the International Committee of the Red Cross.

Sherry Rehman is the president and founding chair of the Jinnah Institute, a nonpartisan public policy think tank committed to the strengthening of democracy, governance and an independent national security project in Pakistan. She co-chairs several track-two strategic dialogues with India, and is convener of a similar institutionalized dialogue process between Pakistan and Afghanistan. She is vice president of the Pakistan People's Party. She has served as Pakistan's ambassador to the United States (2011–13), federal minister for information and broadcasting (2008–09), and ranking member of the National Security Committee in the Parliament, where she was a member of Parliament in the National Assembly from the Pakistan People's Party. As a parliamentarian, she has championed bills to empower and protect women, guarantee an open media environment, and prevent the misuse of blasphemy laws. A former journalist, she was the first Pakistani media person to be recognized by the U.K. House of Lords for independent journalism at the Annual British Muslim Ceremony in 2002. She is one of the founding members of the Human Rights Commission of Pakistan, and has been the recipient of several international awards such as Democracy's Hero by the International Republican Institute and the Jeanne Kirkpatrick Award. *Foreign Policy* magazine recognized her as one of its top Global Thinkers in 2011, and *Newsweek* (Pakistan) labeled her "Pakistan's Most Important Woman" on its cover the same year. For her services to Pakistan, she has been awarded the state's highest civil award, the Nishan-i-Imtiaz in March 2013.

Barnett Rubin is a senior fellow and associate director of New York University Center on International Cooperation's Afghanistan Pakistan Regional Program. During 1994–2000 he was director of the Center for Preventive Action, and director, peace and conflict studies, at the Council on Foreign Relations in New York. From April 2009 until October 2013, he was the senior adviser to the special representative of the president for Afghanistan and Pakistan in the U.S. Department of State. In November-December 2001, he served as special advisor to the UN special representative of the secretary general for Afghanistan, during the negotiations that produced the Bonn Agreement. He received a Ph.D. (1982) and M.A. (1976) from the University of Chicago and a B.A. (1972) from Yale University. He is the author, most recently, of *Afghanistan from the Cold War Through the War on Terror*. Previous books include: *Blood on the Doorstep: The Politics of Preventing Violent Conflict* and *The Fragmentation of Afghanistan: State Formation and Collapse in the International System*.

Najam Aziz Sethi is an alumnus of Clare College, Cambridge University, where he did a stint as Eric Lane Fellow in 2011. He is the recipient of three international media awards, including the Golden Pen for Freedom from the World Association of Newspapers, and the Hilal i Pakistan, the country's highest civil award. He was a federal minister in 1996 and chief minister of Punjab Province in 2013. His interest in cricket led to serve as chairman of the Pakistan Cricket Board 2013–14 and president of the International Cricket Council 2015–16. His media commitments remain as editor in chief of *The Friday Times* and host of *Aapas Ki Baat*, Pakistan's most authoritative and popular political talk show on GEO television.

James Shinn is is lecturer at Princeton University's School of Engineering and Applied Science, chairman of Teneo Intelligence, and CEO of Predata. After careers on Wall Street and in Silicon Valley, he served as national intelligence officer for East Asia at the Central Intelligence Agency and as assistant secretary of defense for Asia at the Pentagon. He serves on the advisory boards of CQS, a London-based hedge fund, and Kensho, a Cambridge-based financial analytics firm.

Nobuaki Tanaka was the UN under-secretary-general for disarmament affairs from 2006 until 2007. Over a forty-year career in the foreign service, he served as Japanese ambassador to Pakistan and Turkey. He was assistant-director-general (management and administration) for UNESCO, and was formerly spokesman and deputy director general for American affairs and policy coordination in the Japanese Ministry of Foreign Affairs. He was senior fellow at the Nakasone Institute and a professor at Doshisha Women's College and lecturer at Waseda University.

Ann Wilkens is a member of the advisory board of the Afghan Analysts Network (AAN). Her background is in journalism and diplomacy and she was posted to Islamabad as Sweden's ambassador to Pakistan and Afghanistan between 2003 and 2007. Between 2009 and 2011, she was the president of the Swedish Committee for Afghanistan and between 2012 and 2014, she chaired the Swedish chapter of Transparency International. She now works as an independent political analyst.

Moeed W. Yusuf is director of South Asia programs at the U.S. Institute of Peace (USIP). His current research focuses on youth and democratic institutions in Pakistan, policy options to mitigate militancy in Pakistan and the South Asian region in general, and the U.S. role in South Asian crisis management. Before joining USIP, he was a fellow at the Frederick S. Pardee Center for the Study of the Longer-Range Future at Boston University, and concurrently a research fellow at the Mossavar-Rahmani Center at Harvard Kennedy School. Yusuf taught in Boston University's Political Science and International Relations Departments as a senior teaching fellow in 2009. He had previously taught at the defense and strategic studies department at Quaid-e-Azam University, Pakistan. He is the editor, most recently, of *Pakistan's Counter-terrorism Challenge; Insurgency and Counterinsurgency in South Asia: From a Peacebuilding Lens;* and *South Asia 2060: Envisioning Regional Futures.* He holds a master's degree in international relations and PhD in political science from Boston University.

Mosharraf Zaidi, *Principal Investigator,* currently leads Alif Ailaan, a political campaign to help address Pakistan's education crisis. Previously, he has held senior positions with governments and various international organizations. Until January 2013, he was the principal adviser to the foreign minister of Pakistan. His responsibilities at the ministry include working on Pakistan's key strategic relationships, and establishing the ministry's public diplomacy unit. Over the course of his career as a government adviser, he has supported local government reform in New York City (for the New York City Council), administrative reform in the Government of the Punjab (for the Chief Minister of the Punjab), and numerous reform efforts, including technology policy, higher education, and capital markets reform for the Government of Pakistan. He has also advised the United Nations, the European Union, the World Bank, the Asian Development Bank, the U.K. Government's DFID, and the Danish and Swiss governments on policy issues in Afghanistan, Pakistan, and the South Asia region. He writes a regular column for *The News* in Pakistan. His writing has also appeared in a variety of other publications, including *Al-Shorouk in Egypt* (in Arabic), the *New York Times, Foreign Policy, The Nation,* the *Times of India,* the *National,* and the *Wall Street Journal.* He is a frequent contributor to television and radio, including CNN, BBC, Al-Jazeera English, National Public Radio, PTV, GEO News and Capital TV.

Anthony Zinni is the former commander-in-chief of the United States Central Command. He retired from active service in the United States Marine Corps in 2000. He has participated in presidential diplomatic missions to Somalia, Pakistan, Ethiopia, and Eritrea, and State Department missions involving the Israeli-Palestinian conflict and conflicts in Indonesia and the Philippines. He sits on numerous corporate, philanthropic, and advisory boards, and has lectured widely on military affairs, national security, and foreign policy. He is a professor of military science at Old Dominion University. He holds a bachelor's degree in economics from Villanova University; a master's degree in international relations from Salvae Regina College; a master's degree in business from Central Michigan University; and honorary doctorates from Villanova University, William and Mary College, and the Maine Maritime Academy. His most recent book on national security policy is *Before the First Shots are Fired: How America Can Win or Lose Off the Battlefield*. His other books include *Battle Ready*, a memoir co-authored with Tom Clancy; *The Battle For Peace: A Frontline Vision of America's Power;* and *Leading the Charge.*